HAWAI'I'S
New Best
Local Desserts

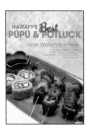

HAWAI'I'S
New Best
Local
Desserts

Jean Watanabe Hee

Mutual Publishing

Library of Congress Control Number: 2013944383

ISBN: 978-1939487-11-7

First Printing, September 2013
Second Printing, September 2014

Mutual Publishing, LLC
1215 Center Street, Suite 210
Honolulu, Hawai'i 96816
Ph: 808-732-1709 / Fax: 808-734-4094
email: info@mutualpublishing.com
www.mutualpublishing.com

Printed in Korea

To our Popo, Ellen Hee,
who celebrated her 97th birthday this year. She
was also honored this year when she was named
the 2013 Model Chinese Mother of the Year.
She deserves all the accolades.
Thank you, Popo, for your loving support
and prayers all these years.

Table of Contents

COOKIES & BARS

ASSORTED TREATS

Acknowledgments

I am so grateful to my good friends and neighbors, Ruby Saito and Evelyn Shiraki, who were so helpful and generous in sharing recipes with me. Whenever they tasted a delicious dessert made by friends at any type of gathering they would ask for the recipe. This is such a local thing. We all do it, and most people are more than happy to share. I appreciate all those people sharing, and their names are often acknowledged with the recipes they shared.

Ruby and Evelyn both went a step further. Since they had tasted it and I didn't, they often made the dessert so I had a sample when I got the recipe. That really helped me.

Introduction

It has been twelve years since *Hawai'i's Best Local Desserts* was published with many favorite recipes from family gatherings and potlucks, and it has been popular ever since. Many great, easy, and tasty desserts are still being prepared from this cookbook.

Since then I have accumulated and tested new recipes (some have been around for a number of years), and so this second *Hawai'i's New Best Desserts* cookbook is a wonderful collection of recipes which cannot be found in the first.

There are still many quick-and-easy recipes for all you busy people out there, but I have included more "from scratch" desserts by request. And I have made the directions easier to follow. For example, in testing and writing out the recipe for chocolate cake I added more information from the original recipe that I thought would help first-time cake-layer bakers. The recipe appears difficult, but it's not. The cake is moist and delicious, and your friends will be impressed.

I also did the opposite. After sampling my sister-in law's (Evelyn Hee) apple pie, I had to make it. I loved the fresh taste of the apples that had a hint of lemon and orange. So I simplified the complicated "from scratch" recipe to make it easier for anyone to prepare. Even though I had never made a fresh apple pie before I was determined to test it and share it with you, and I found it wasn't too difficult, so I hope you try it.

If you like carrot cake, the "from scratch" carrot cake shared by Ruth P is another great recipe. I've never cared for carrot cake, because it tends to be too sweet for me, but this one I liked very much. I have made it several times for potlucks. Everyone raves about it, even my friend Roy N., a discriminating carrot cake enthusiast. He and his wife, Lorraine, gave it a thumbs up.

Included are many easy recipes that you can use successfully make. Try making Two Bite Easy Scones, Super Easy Popovers, or Chocolate Cherry Cake.

As you can see, I love this second desserts cookbook. There are so many great recipes for you to try. It is a complement to the first desserts cookbook, and it will find a place right beside it on your shelf.

Cakes
& Breads

5 Minute Chocolate Mug Cake

Yield: 1 serving

4 Tablespoons flour
4 Tablespoons sugar
2 Tablespoons unsweetened cocoa
1 egg
3 Tablespoons milk
3 Tablespoons oil
Dash vanilla extract

Add dry ingredients in large "microsafe" coffee mug; mix well. Add egg; mix thoroughly. Pour in milk, oil and vanilla and mix well. Place mug in microwave and cook, uncovered, on high for 3 minutes. (Adjust cooking time as necessary.) Remove and cool slightly. Tip out onto a plate.

- **NOTE:** *Recipe shared by Gwen Amai Murai. Gwen willingly shared recipes from her collection. This unique cake for one really works. While cooking, cake will rise over top of mug but will not overflow. My large coffee mug that I use is a 2-cup size mug.*

- **VARIATION:** *Mix in 3 Tablespoons chocolate chips, if desired.*

- **SUGGESTION:** *Cut cake in half, serve with ice cream for a quick and easy dessert for two.*

Alice's Famous Biscuit

Yield: 24 servings

½ cup butter (1 block)
6 cups flour
¾ cup sugar
4 Tablespoons baking powder
4 eggs, slightly beaten
2 cups milk

Preheat oven 400°F. While oven is preheating, place butter in 9 x 13-inch pan and place in oven to melt. When butter melts remove from oven and set aside.

In large bowl, mix together flour, sugar, and baking powder. Add eggs and milk and mix together until just blended. Scoop dough using large spoon and place in pan. Bake for 25 to 30 minutes until brown. Check for doneness. Cut into desired portions.

> HINT: *Delicious just by itself but it also makes a great strawberry shortcake.*
>
> NOTE: *Recipe shared by Alice Ichinose. Alice's husband, Gary, is my classmate (Hilo High School 1957).*

Angel Tunnel Cake

Yield: about 20 servings

1 box Duncan Hines® Angel Food Cake mix (16 oz.)
2 teaspoons coconut extract, divided
2 containers Cool Whip® (8 oz. each)
½ container fresh strawberries (half of 16 oz. box), washed, hulled
    and chopped
4 drops red food coloring

Prepare angel food cake according to box instructions, adding 1 teaspoon coconut extract to batter. Bake in tube pan according to baking instructions. Hang pan upside down until completely cooled (about ½ hour). Loosen edges carefully with flat knife and remove cake.

Cut off ⅓ from top of cake; set aside. To make tunnel, use a sharp knife to carefully hollow out the remaining ⅔ cake leaving a ½-inch shell. Tear removed cake into 1-inch cubes.

Mix 2 containers Cool Whip® with 1 teaspoon coconut extract. Add strawberries and cake cubes and mix together. Remove 2 cups and mix in red color. Spoon into tunnel; replace the ⅓ part back onto cake. Use the remaining Cool Whip® to frost the cake. Decorate with strawberries.

> 🍰 **NOTE:** *Jeri Barnes shared this popular dessert which she often serves to her guests. She suggested using coconut extract which adds a certain flavor that improves the cake box taste.*

Cakes & Breads

Apple Spice Cake

Yield: 24 servings

4 cups apples, cored and diced (Fuji, Granny Smith or Gala)
1 cup sugar

2 cups flour
2 teaspoons baking soda
2 teaspoons cinnamon
½ teaspoon nutmeg
½ teaspoon salt
1 cup walnuts, chopped; or sliced almonds

2 eggs
½ cup canola oil
2 teaspoons vanilla

In large bowl, combine apples and sugar; set aside.

Sift together flour, baking soda, cinnamon, nutmeg and salt. Add to apples; mix together. Add walnuts or almonds and toss to mix well. Set aside.

Whisk together eggs, oil and vanilla until smooth. Add to apple mixture and stir until well-blended. Spread evenly in buttered 9 x 13-inch pan and bake at 350°F for 45 to 60 minutes, or until toothpick inserted in center comes out clean.

> **NOTE:** *Very tasty and moist! Berenice Lum who shared this recipe says she uses slightly more apples and almonds. She also uses freshly grated nutmeg and reduces it to ¼ teaspoon. Half of the amount of flour can be whole wheat flour, if desired.*

Avocado Cake

Yield: three 8-inch cake pans

¾ cup shortening (e.g. Crisco®)
2 cups sugar
3 eggs

2⅔ cups sifted flour
¾ teaspoon cinnamon
¾ teaspoon allspice
¾ teaspoon salt

1¼ teaspoons baking soda
¾ cup sour milk*
1½ cups ripe avocado, mashed
½ cup chopped dates
¾ cup macadamia nuts, chopped
¾ cup raisins

¼ cup sugar mixed with 1 teaspoon cinnamon for sprinkling

In large bowl, beat together shortening and sugar until fluffy; add eggs one at a time, beating after each egg. In medium bowl, sift together flour, cinnamon, allspice and salt.

Dissolve baking soda in sour milk. Into large bowl of beaten shortening mixture, mix in avocado, sifted flour and spices, adding alternately with sour milk; mix well. Fold dates, nuts and raisins into batter. Pour batter into 3 greased and floured 8 x 8-inch pans. Sprinkle desired amount of sugar/cinnamon over. Bake at 350°F for 35 to 40 minutes. Check for doneness with toothpick.

*To make sour milk, mix in 1 teaspoon vinegar or lemon juice to 1 cup whole or 2 percent milk. Let sit for 10 to 15 minutes. The milk should begin to curdle slightly. So for ¾ cup sour milk, I added about ¾ teaspoon vinegar to ¾ cup milk.

> ✎ NOTE: *Thanks to my good friend, Ruby Saito, who is always on the lookout for avocado recipes. She got this recipe from a friend via Maui. I used aluminum 8 x 8-inch pans from Longs® sold in packs of 3 which made this very convenient for me.*

Butter Coffee Cake

Yield: 24 servings

1 box yellow cake mix (18.25 oz.)
½ cup butter (1 block), melted
4 eggs (divided)
1 box cream cheese (8 oz.), softened

2¼ cups powdered sugar, divided

Beat together cake mix, butter and 2 eggs until blended. Spread mixture evenly in greased 9 x 13-inch pan. Set aside.

Beat cream cheese, adding 2 cups of the powdered sugar. Add 2 eggs; beat until well blended. Pour on top of cake mix mixture. Bake at 350°F for 30 to 35 minutes. Sprinkle with remaining sugar when taken from oven. Cut when cool. Refrigerate any left over.

> 🍰 NOTE: *Easy to make and very tasty. A little unusual texture but I liked the combination of the heavier cake and the cream cheese topping.*

Amy's Sponge Cake

Yield: 12 servings

Orange zest from 2 oranges (about 2 to 3 teaspoons)
½ cup fresh orange juice (about 2 oranges)

10 eggs, separated
1½ teaspoons cream of tartar
1 cup sugar, separated

1 cup cake flour
2½ teaspoons baking powder
½ teaspoon salt
½ cup vegetable oil
1 teaspoon vanilla

Finely grate orange skin for orange zest; set aside. Squeeze oranges for juice; set aside.

In medium bowl, beat egg whites, cream of tartar and ½ cup of the sugar on high speed for 7 minutes; set aside.

In large bowl, sift cake flour, remaining ½ cup of sugar, baking powder and salt. Add oil, egg yolks, vanilla, orange juice and orange zest and beat on medium speed for 15 minutes. Fold in egg white; pour into ungreased tube pan. Bake at 325°F for 35 to 40 minutes or until top is brown. (Do not open oven door while baking.) Check for doneness with pick or skewer. Invert over bottle and cool over 2 hours. Slide knife around sides and center to release cake.

> ✎ NOTE: *This is my favorite cake made by my sister-in-law, Amy Hee. It is silky smooth and moist. Amy said the large 10 fl. oz. Worcestershire Sauce bottle is a perfect size to place the inverted tube pan. She also recommended that the cake cool away from wind.*

Breakfast Bread Pudding

Yield: 24 servings

1 cup sugar
2 cups milk
½ cup butter (1 block)
1 teaspoon vanilla
6 eggs, whisked well

12 mini croissants (stale is better)
1 box cream cheese (8 oz.)
1 can apple pie filling (21 oz.)
Cinnamon for sprinkling

In sauce pan, combine sugar, milk and butter. Heat on medium-low and bring to slight boil, stirring occasionally. Remove from heat; cool. Add vanilla and well-whisked eggs; mix thoroughly.

Spray 9 x 13-inch pan with non-stick spray. Cut croissants in half lengthwise and line pan with half the amount. Slice cream cheese in thin slices and line over croissants. Layer remaining croissants over. Pour milk mixture over croissants. Spread apple pie filling over. Sprinkle cinnamon over all. Bake at 350°F for 30 minutes. Serve either hot or cold.

🖉 **NOTE:** *It's called a breakfast pudding but I also consider it a fantastic pastry dessert. Gwen Murai sent me this great recipe. Gwen got it from Pearl N. Takahashi who got it from Elsie Higa Miike. We're all classmates from Hilo High class of 1957. I am so thankful for all the sharing of recipes.*

🖉 **NOTE:** *If you're out of milk, Pearl used one can evaporated milk and added enough water to total 2 cups.*

🖉 **SUGGESTION:** *Our Popo prefers peaches to apples so I have also used peach pie filling in place of the apple pie filling and eliminated the cinnamon. You can also substitute with blueberry pie filling, if desired.*

Chantilly Cake

Yield: 8 to 10 servings

1²/₃ cups sifted cake flour
1½ cups sugar, divided
¾ teaspoon baking soda
¾ teaspoon salt

3 eggs, separated
1 square unsweetened chocolate(1 oz.), melted in microwave 45 to
    50 seconds
⅓ cup vegetable oil
1 cup whole milk, divided

Generously grease two 9 x 9-inch cake pans. Preheat oven to 350°F.

In large bowl, sift together cake flour, 1 cup of the sugar, baking soda and salt; set aside.

Beat egg whites until frothy. Gradually beat in remaining ½ cup of the sugar until soft peaks form; set aside.

Add chocolate, oil and ½ cup of the milk to the large bowl of flour mixture. Beat one minute on medium speed. Add egg yolks and remaining ½ cup milk. Beat one minute until smooth. With rubber spatula, gently but thoroughly fold in egg white mixture. Pour into cake pans. Bake for 30 to 35 minutes. Cool in pans on racks for 30 minutes. Remove from pans. (If necessary, use a flat knife to carefully help separate cake from pan.) Use a sharp knife to split cake layers through the middle into four squares.

Cakes & Breads

CREAM FILLING:

¼ cup sugar
4 teaspoons cornstarch
⅛ teaspoon salt
1 egg, slightly beaten
1 cup whole milk
1½ teaspoons butter
½ teaspoon vanilla extract

In saucepan, combine sugar, cornstarch and salt. Add egg; blend well with wooden spoon. Stir in milk slowly. Cook over medium heat, stirring constantly, until mixture comes to boil and thickens. Remove from heat and stir in butter and vanilla. Chill for 30 minutes. Spread a third of the mixture between each layer. Refrigerate cake.

CHANTILLY FROSTING:

1 can evaporated milk (12 oz.)
1½ cups sugar
¾ cup butter (1½ blocks)
4 large egg yolks
1½ teaspoons vanilla extract
¼ cup pecans, chopped and toasted

In saucepan, combine milk, sugar, butter and egg yolks. Cook, stirring constantly, over medium heat for 15 minutes, or until mixture thickens. (Must be thickened enough so that it will not slide off cake.) Remove from heat and stir in vanilla. Chill 1 hour covered with waxed paper directly on surface. Frost cake and sprinkle with chopped pecans. Chill for 2 hours or more before serving.

🖎 HINT: *As frosting begins to thicken, lower heat slightly, stirring constantly.*

🖎 NOTE: *Very delicious! Very similar to Liliha's Chantilly Cake. Paulette Tam shared this recipe. It looks difficult, but if you take it step by step it's manageable.*

Corn Bread

Yield: 24 to 30 servings

3 cups Bisquick®
1 cup sugar
1 teaspoon baking powder
¾ cup + 1 Tablespoon cornmeal
1 cup butter (2 blocks), melted and cooled slightly
3 eggs, beaten
1½ cups milk

In large bowl, mix together Bisquick®, sugar, baking powder and cornmeal.

In another bowl, beat eggs and mix in milk and melted butter. Add milk mixture into dry mixture and mix until blended. Pour in greased 9 x 13-inch pan. Bake at 350°F for 25 to 30 minutes.

> NOTE: *Shared by Ruby Saito whose mother liked this dense, slighty gritty corn bread and recommended it to me. This is another corn bread recipe that you may want to try. I did and liked it very much.*

Granny Smith Apple Cake

12 servings

¾ cup pecans, chopped
3 cups flour, divided
2 cups sugar, divided
2 teaspoons cinnamon
4 large Granny Smith apples, peeled, cored, and sliced
1 Tablespoon baking powder
1 teaspoon salt
4 large eggs
½ cup vegetable oil
½ cup unsalted butter (1 block), melted
¼ cup orange juice
2 teaspoons vanilla extract

Spray a 10-inch removable-bottom tube pan with nonstick spray. Sprinkle pecans evenly on bottom of pan.

In large bowl, mix 2 Tablespoons of the flour, ¼ cup of the sugar, and cinnamon. Add apples and toss to combine.

In another large bowl, mix the rest of the remaining flour and 1¾ cup sugar, baking powder, and salt. Add eggs, oil, butter, orange juice and vanilla. Beat until batter is smooth. Pour half of the batter (about 2 cups) into pan. Top with half of apple mixture. Spoon remaining batter over apples and top with remaining apples, Placing them ¼ inch in from the tube and sides of pan.

Bake at 350°F for 1 hour and 20 minutes, or until toothpick inserted in the center of the cake comes out clean. Cool cake in pan on wire rack for 30 minutes. Run a paring knife around the sides and center of cake and turn cake out onto wire rack. Invert cake onto another rack to cool, apple side up.

> ✎ HINT: *Measure 3 cups flour first. Then take 2 Tablespoons flour. Use a vegetable peeler to peel apples.*
>
> ✎ NOTE: *Got this recipe from Karen Hamada's mom, Ellen Hamada. Jennifer and I really like this apple cake.*

Carrot Cake

Yield: 24 servings

1½ cups flour
1⅓ cups sugar
½ cup sweetened flaked coconut
⅓ cup pecans, chopped
2 teaspoons baking soda
1 teaspoon salt
2 teaspoons cinnamon
2 eggs
3 Tablespoons canola oil
2 cups grated carrot (about 3 large carrots)
1 can crushed pineapple (20 oz.), drained

In large bowl, combine flour, sugar, coconut, pecans, baking soda, salt and cinnamon; stir well with whisk. Set aside. In small bowl, beat eggs; add oil. Stir well. Add egg mixture, grated carrot and pineapple into flour mixture and mix well together. Spoon batter into 9 x 13-inch pan coated with cooking spray. Bake at 350°F for 35 minutes or until wooden toothpick in center comes out clean. Cool completely.

FROSTING:

2 Tablespoons butter, softened
1 box cream cheese (8 oz.), ⅓ less fat, softened
2 to 3 cups powdered sugar (adjust to taste), sifted
2 teaspoons vanilla
Grated carrot and pecans for garnish (optional)

In large bowl, beat butter and cream cheese at medium speed until smooth. Add powdered sugar and vanilla and beat just until smooth. Spread frosting over top of cake. Garnish each serving with grated carrot and/or pecan halves, if desired.

> ✎ NOTE: *Ruth Prinzivalli prepared this carrot cake to celebrate a birthday and all loved it. What made it even better was that it was a lighter carrot cake with less than a third of the fat. I've made it several times with good favorable reviews from carrot cake lovers.*

Moist Prune Cake

Yield: 24 servings

1 box spice cake mix (18.25 oz.)
1 box instant vanilla pudding (3 oz.)
1 cup prunes, cooked and chopped
1 cup prune juice
½ cup butter (1 block), melted
4 eggs
1 teaspoon baking soda
1 teaspoon vanilla

Mix all ingredients; beat for 3 minutes. Pour into greased 9 x 13-inch pan. Bake at 350°F for 40 to 45 minutes.

> ✎ **NOTE:** *Cover prunes with water and simmer about 15 minutes or until softened. My daughter liked the cake in spite of having prunes in it.*

Super Easy Popovers

Yield: 12 popovers

2 eggs
1 cup cold milk
1 cup Gold Medal Wondra® quick mixing flour
1 teaspoon salt

Preheat oven 450°F. Generously grease muffin pan.

Beat eggs with a fork and add milk; beat together. Mix in flour and salt; mix until lumps are gone. Pour into greased muffin pan. Bake at 450°F for 20 to 25 minutes, or until browned. Then reduce oven to 350°F; bake 15 minutes more.

Chocolate Cake

Yield: 16 servings

2 cups flour
2 cups sugar
¾ cup unsweetened cocoa
1 teaspoon salt
1 teaspoon baking powder
2 teaspoons baking soda

1 cup vegetable oil
1 cup hot coffee
1 cup milk
2 eggs, slightly beaten
1 teaspoon vanilla

Preheat oven 325°F. Grease and flour two round 9-inch cake pans.

Sift together dry ingredients. Add oil, coffee and milk; beat at medium speed for 2 minutes. Add eggs and vanilla; beat 2 more minutes. Pour into cake pans. Bake for 25 to 30 minutes or until toothpick inserted in center comes out clean. Cool on wire racks for 15 minutes. Turn cakes out on rack and cool completely.

FROSTING:

1 cup milk
5 Tablespoons flour
½ cup butter (1 block), softened
½ cup Crisco®
1 cup sugar
1 teaspoon vanilla

Combine milk and flour in saucepan; cook on medium low, stirring constantly, about 10 minutes, until thick. Cover and refrigerate.

In medium mixing bowl, beat together butter and Crisco®. Add sugar and vanilla; beat until creamy. Add chilled milk and flour mixture; beat for 5 to 10 minutes.

If necessary, use a serrated knife to trim off any domed part from tops of cake. To frost cake, carefully separate cake from wire rack and place one cake layer, top side down, on a serving plate. Frost evenly on top of cake layer. Place the other layer, top side down, on the first layer. Spread frosting over top and sides.

> 🍰 **NOTE:** *Great tasting cake! Very moist. I found that Williams-Sonoma Gold Touch® nonstick round cake pans are best for easy baking. Do grease and flour, however. The cakes come out even on top and turn out easily.*

Chocolate Cherry Cake

Yield: 24 servings

4 eggs
1 cup oil
1 box Duncan Hines® Devil's Food cake mix (16.5 oz.)
1 can cherry pie filling (21 oz.)

In large bowl, beat eggs. Add oil; beat together. Add cake mix; mix well. Fold cherry pie filling into batter. Pour into greased 9 x 13-inch pan. Bake at 325°F for approximately 40 minutes or until done. Test for doneness with toothpick inserted in middle.

> 🍰 **NOTE:** *Very moist and delicious! Another recipe shared by Pearl N. Takahashi.*

Cheesecake

Yield: 24 to 30 servings

CRUST:

20 to 24 Oreo® cookies, finely crushed (about 2¾ cups)
3 Tablespoons butter, melted

Mix together crumbs and butter. Press into bottom of greased 9 x 13-inch pan. Set aside.

FILLING:

5 boxes cream cheese (8 oz. each), softened
1 cup sugar
3 Tablespoons flour
1 Tablespoon vanilla
1 cup sour cream
4 eggs

TOPPING:

1 can cherry pie filling (21 oz.)

Preheat oven 325°F.

Beat together cream cheese and sugar. Add flour, vanilla and sour cream; beat together until well-blended. Add eggs one at a time, mixing on low after each just until blended. Pour over crust. Bake at 325°F for 40 to 45 minutes. Cool completely. Refrigerate 4 hours. Top with cherry pie filling.

> 🍰 NOTE: *Evelyn Shiraki shared this cheese cake recipe. It has a been a big hit at many potlucks since then. Delicious! Ruby Saito experimented using mint center Oreo® cookies and I like that version also.*
>
> 🍰 NOTE: *For easier handling, Evelyn lines the pan with foil, with ends extending over sides of pan, before pressing the crust mixture onto bottom of pan. After cheesecake has been refrigerated, lift cheesecake from pan using foil "handles." Cut into pieces. Garnish with cherry pie filling just before serving.*

Chocolate Oreo® Cheesecake

Yield: 36 pieces

36 Oreo® cookies
1 box instant chocolate pudding (3.9 oz.)
1 box instant vanilla pudding (3.4 oz.)
3 cups milk

2 boxes cream cheese (8 oz. each), softened
¾ cup sugar
2 eggs
1 teaspoon vanilla
Cool Whip® for topping

Whisk chocolate and vanilla pudding with milk until thickened. Refrigerate to set.

Beat together cream cheese and sugar. Add 1 egg; beat. Add second egg and vanilla; beat together. Line 3 cupcake pans with cupcake liners. Place an Oreo® cookie into each. Spoon one tablespoonful of cheesecake mixture over each cookie. Bake at 350°F for 15 minutes. Cool.

Place heaping tablespoonful of pudding onto cheesecake. Refrigerate. Just before serving, top with Cool Whip®.

Easy Chocolate Frosting

Yield: enough for 1 dozen cupcakes

1 container chocolate frosting (1 pound) e.g. Duncan Hines®
1 teaspoon vanilla
½ teaspoon instant coffee

Stir vanilla and instant coffee into frosting until smooth.

Chocolate Surprise

Yield: 30 servings

1 box cream cheese (8 oz.), softened
½ cup sugar
1 egg

1 box Duncan Hines® Devil's Food Cake Mix (18.25 oz.)
1 box instant vanilla pudding (3 oz.)
3 eggs
½ cup oil
1 cup water
1 cup chocolate chips, or use less (optional)

Beat cream cheese and sugar together. Add 1 egg and beat well. Set aside.

Mix together cake mix, instant vanilla pudding, 3 eggs, oil and water at low speed until moistened. Then beat at medium speed until well blended (about 2 minutes).

Pour half of cake batter into greased 9 x 13-inch pan. Cover with cream cheese batter. Carefully spread rest of chocolate batter over. Sprinkle desired amount of chocolate chips over. Bake at 325°F for 45 to 50 minutes or until done.

> ✎ NOTE: *Winifred Hee shared this recipe that she got from a friend. She said it was good. After I made it, I agree. It is good! And my neighbors also agree. It tastes great with or without the chocolate chips.*

Cakes & Breads

Cocoa Mochi Cake

Yield: 2 loaf pans

4½ cups mochiko
4½ cups sugar
1 Tablespoon baking soda
5 Tablespoons cocoa powder

5 eggs
1 can coconut milk (13.5 oz.)
1 cup evaporated milk
1 Tablespoon vanilla
½ cup butter (1 block), melted

In large bowl, combine mochiko, sugar, baking soda and cocoa powder; set aside.

In another bowl, beat eggs. Add coconut milk, 1 cup evaporated milk, vanilla and melted butter; mix together.

Make a well in center of mochiko mixture and pour liquid into center, stirring from center (like a whirlpool) gradually moving outward until batter is smooth. Pour into 2 greased 9 x 5-inch loaf pans and bake at 375°F for 75 to 90 minutes. Check for doneness. Cool. Cut into pieces with plastic knife.

✎ NOTE: *Melt butter first so it'll be cool before mixing together. Note that the recipe calls for 1 cup evaporated milk and not 1 can.*

✎ SUGGESTION: *Leftover cocoa mochi cake may be refrigerated or frozen. Microwave for a little while (time varies depending on amount) to get it warm and moist.*

Coconut Cake

Yield: 24 servings

1 box yellow cake mix (18.5 oz.)
1 box instant vanilla pudding (3.4 oz.)
½ cup vegetable oil
4 eggs
½ teaspoon vanilla
1 can coconut milk (13.5 oz.)

GLAZE:

2 cups powdered sugar, sifted
⅓ cup water
1 teaspoon vanilla
2 Tablespoons butter, melted

Preheat oven 350°F. Grease 9 x 13-inch pan.

Beat together all cake ingredients (except coconut milk). When combined, mix in coconut milk. Pour into greased pan and bake for 35 to 40 minutes.

While cake is baking, mix together glaze ingredients until well blended. When cake is done, poke holes in hot cake with a fork. Spoon glaze evenly over.

> ✎ **NOTE:** *Recipe was given to Evelyn Shiraki from her friend and shared with others. The cake is easy to prepare and tasty.*

Cream Puff Cake

Yield: 24 servings

CRUST:

1 cup water
½ cup butter or margarine (1 block)
1 cup flour
4 eggs

Boil water and margarine on medium heat. Add flour all at once. Quick-ly stir with wooden spoon until mixture comes off the sides of the pot. Place in large mixing bowl. Cool about 10 minutes. Add eggs, one at a time, beating well after each one. Spread into greased 9 x 13-inch pan. Bake at 400°F for 30 minutes. Set aside to cool.

FILLING:

1 box cream cheese (8 oz.), softened to room temperature
2 boxes instant pudding (3.9 oz. each), flavor of your choice
2½ cups milk

TOPPING:

1 container Cool Whip® (8 oz.)
Chocolate syrup (optional) for drizzling

Beat cream cheese until fluffy. Add pudding and milk. Continue to beat at low moderate speed until smooth, scraping sides with spatula to help smooth out lumps. Spread mixture onto cooled crust. Spread Cool Whip® over and drizzle chocolate syrup, if desired.

> NOTE: *Thank you, Keith Won. This is a big favorite of my family. They think it's the greatest! Keith said the recipe originally came from Kandyce who made it with chocolate pudding with caramel chips. I made it with chocolate pudding since I had that in my cupboard and everyone loved it!*

Fresh Blueberry Muffins

Yield: 30 muffins

1 cup butter or margarine (2 blocks), softened
1½ cups sugar
3 cups + 3 Tablespoons flour
2¾ teaspoons baking powder
¾ teaspoon salt
¾ teaspoon nutmeg or cinnamon

3 eggs
1 cup + 2 Tablespoons milk
¾ teaspoons vanilla
2¾ cups fresh blueberries

Beat together butter and sugar until light and fluffy. In another bowl, sift together flour, baking powder, salt and nutmeg.

Starting and ending with an egg, alternate adding eggs and flour mixture to butter mixture, beating until mixed well. Add milk and vanilla and mix together. Stir in blueberries. Pour into paper-lined muffin pans about 5/8 full. Bake at 375°F for 20 minutes or until done. Remove from oven and let sit for a few minutes before turning them out onto a cooling rack.

> NOTE: *While visiting Hilo, Kay Yanagihara brought over her fresh blueberry muffins. She always bakes a special treat whenever I visit and these muffins were especially fluffy and tasty. I had to ask her for her recipe.*

Hawaiian Pineapple Mango Bread

Yield: 6 to 8 servings

- -

2 cups flour
¼ cup sugar
½ teaspoon salt
2 teaspoons cinnamon
2 teaspoons baking soda

¾ cup vegetable oil
3 eggs
1 can crushed pineapple in heavy syrup (8.25 oz.)
2 cups mango, diced
½ cup nuts, chopped

Sift together all dry ingredients in large mixing bowl. Mix well and add oil, eggs and pineapple. Beat well. Add mango and nuts; Mix together. Pour into well greased and floured loaf pan. Bake at 350°F for 1 hour, or until skewer inserted in center comes out cleanly.

> ✑ NOTE: *Moist and delicious! The crushed pineapple really tastes great with the mango. I used frozen mango with good results.*

Fruit Cake

Yield: 3 small loaf pans

1 box cream cheese (8 oz.), room temperature
1 cup butter (2 blocks), room temperature
1½ cups sugar
1½ teaspoons vanilla
4 eggs, room temperature
2½ cups flour
1½ teaspoons baking powder
½ cup nuts, chopped
1 cup fruit cake mix (or dried cranberry, blueberry, etc.)

Beat together cream cheese, butter and sugar well. Add vanilla and eggs; beat together. Add flour and baking powder; mix thoroughly with a heavy spoon. Stir in nuts and fruit. Spray 3 small loaf pans (2 pound pans, 8 x 3¾ x 2⅜) with non-stick cooking spray. Spoon batter into pans. Bake at 325°F for 55 minutes.

> 🖎 **NOTE:** *A very light fruit cake which I really liked. This is not the traditional type but one that is easier to make and enjoy. More like a pound cake with fruit cake mixed in to celebrate the holidays.*

Jeri's Easy Trifle

Yield: 15 to 20 servings

1 box chocolate cake mix (16.5 oz.), bake according to box directions
2 boxes instant chocolate pudding (3.9 oz. each), prepare according
 to box directions
1 to 2 containers Cool Whip® (8 oz. each)
Oreo® cookies, crushed

OPTIONAL TOPPINGS:

Nuts, chocolate chips, M&M's®, chopped up candies
  (e.g. Andes® Mint candy gives a nice flavor)

Follow cake box directions and bake cake in 9 x 13-inch pan. Cool.

Prepare chocolate pudding as directed. Chill.

Cut cake into ½-inch cubes and place half of the amount in large bowl.* Pat down into bottom of bowl and cover with half of the pudding. Cover with half amount of Cool Whip®. Sprinkle with crushed Oreo® cookies. Repeat layer and add optional toppings. Refrigerate at least 1 hour or until ready to serve.

*Use one large bowl or divide into smaller bowls.

✎ **VARIATION:** *Jeri Goodin likes to experiment with different combinations. For a patriotic fruit variation, use red velvet cake mix, vanilla pudding, Cool Whip® sliced strawberries, blueberries and white chocolate chips.*

✎ *Optional: Use few drops of blue color to Cool Whip®.*

✎ **INTERESTING FOOTNOTE:** *Jeri Goodin was a kindergarten student in my classroom at 'Aikahi Elenebtary School many years ago. She graduated from Le Jardin Academy and is a recent graduate of University of Findlay in Ohio. She and her mother, Kelly, and grandmother, Ruby Saito, all love to bake and create.*

Lemon Cake

Yield: 24 servings

1 box Duncan Hines® Lemon Supreme cake mx (18.25 oz.)
3 eggs
⅓ cup oil
1⅓ cups water
2 boxes lemon instant pudding (3.4 oz. each)
1½ cups milk
Cool Whip® for topping
Lemon zest, freshly grated for sprinkling
Mint (optional) for decorating

Grease and lightly flour 9 x 13-inch pan. Preheat oven to 350°F.

In large bowl, blend cake mix, eggs, oil and water on low speed until moistened. Beat at medium speed for 2 minutes. Pour batter in prepared pan and bake immediately for 32 to 35 minutes. Cool completely when done.

Mix together lemon pudding and milk. Spread pudding over cake. Spread desired amount of Cool Whip® over. Sprinkle lemon zest over. Decorate with mint, if desired. Refrigerate for 2 hours or longer. Serve cold.

✎ **NOTE:** *At a See Dai Do picnic in 2010, James Au won 1st prize for this cake in a bake contest.*

Lemon Apricot Cake

Yield: 20 servings

1 box lemon cake mix (18.25 oz.)
⅓ cup white sugar
¾ cup vegetable oil
1 cup apricot nectar
4 eggs

GLAZE:

2 cups powdered sugar
3 Tablespoons lemon juice (about 2 to 3 lemons)
3 drops vegetable oil (about ⅛ teaspoon)

Grease 10-inch tube or bundt pan. Combine cake mix, sugar, ¾ cup vegetable oil and apricot nectar together. Beat in eggs one at a time, mixing well after each addition. Pour batter into bundt pan. Bake at 325°F for 1 hour. Let cake cool in pan for 10 to 15 minutes.

While cake is cooling, prepare glaze. Combine powdered sugar, lemon juice and oil, mixing until smooth. Use immediately. Drizzle desired amount of glaze over warm cake creating a cobweb-type design.

> 🍰 NOTE: *Very delicious and light. Icing has a light lemon flavor. Another contribution from Evelyn Shiraki.*

Lemon Pineapple Cake

Yield: 24 servings

1 box Duncan Hines® Lemon Supreme Cake Mix (18.25 oz.)
3 eggs
1⅓ cups water
⅓ cup vegetable oil

1 box instant lemon pudding mix (3.4 oz.)
1 box instant vanilla pudding mix (3.4 oz.)
⅔ cup milk
1 container Cool Whip® (8 oz.)

1 can crushed pineapple with juice (20 oz.)
⅓ cup macadamia nuts, finely chopped
⅓ cup grated coconut (optional)

Bake cake according to package directions in greased and floured 9 x 13-inch pan.

While cake is baking, mix together pudding mixes with milk. Fold the whipped cream and instant pudding together. Refrigerate until ready to use.

When cake is done, remove cake from oven and immediately poke holes in the hot cake. Pour pineapple and juice evenly over the top. Cool cake completely.

Frost with pudding mixture. Sprinkle nuts and coconut over.

> ✎ **NOTE:** *People love this cake but if there are any leftover, cake will keep for a week in the refrigerator.*

Lemon Pound Cake

Yield: 2 loaf pans

1 box Duncan Hines® Lemon Supreme cake mix (18.25 oz.)
1 container sour cream (8 oz.)
½ cup butter (1 block), melted
¼ cup oil
1 teaspoon vanilla
4 eggs

Mix all ingredients. Pour into two 9 x 5-inch greased loaf pans. Bake at 325°F for 45 minutes, or until wooden skewer inserted in middle comes out clean.

> 🍰 NOTE: *Quick and easy to make! Evie Hee used my butter pound cake recipe and substituted lemon cake mix to make a moist and lemony pound cake. She also eliminated the ¼ cup sugar the original recipe called for which made this cake less sweet!*

Cream Cheese Frosting

Yield: enough for 1 dozen cupcakes

¼ cup butter (half block), softened
1 box cream cheese (8 oz.), softened
¾ cup powdered sugar (or more)

Beat butter and cream cheese until smooth and fluffy. Add powdered sugar and beat until well blended. Add more powdered sugar if desired.

Lemon Tea Bread

Yield: 12 servings

2¼ cups flour
1½ teaspoons baking powder
½ teaspoon baking soda
¼ teaspoon salt

½ cup butter (1 block)
1 cup sugar
2 eggs
1 cup sour cream
2 teaspoons grated lemon peel

In medium bowl, combine flour, baking powder, baking soda and salt; set aside.

In large glass bowl, melt butter in microwave on high 1 minute. Remove and whisk in sugar, then eggs, sour cream and lemon peel. Add flour mixture, stirring just until blended. Spoon batter into greased 9 x 5-inch loaf pan. Bake at 350°F for 45 to 55 minutes until toothpick inserted in center comes out clean. Cool in pan on wire rack 10 minutes; remove from pan. Cool completely.

> 🖎 **NOTE:** *Berenice Lum made this for St. Ann's as part of the refreshments after the "All Soul's "Service. I found it to be simple and not sweet at all. Wonderful with hot coffee or tea.*

Liliko'i Pound Cake

Yield: 12 servings

1 cup butter (2 blocks), softened
1 cup sugar
4 eggs
1 teaspoon vanilla
1½ cups flour
1 teaspoon baking powder
½ teaspoon salt
¼ cup liliko'i juice

GLAZE:

2 Tablespoons liliko'i juice
1 cup powdered sugar

Beat butter and sugar until fluffy. Beat in eggs one at a time. Add vanilla. Set aside.

In another bowl, combine flour, baking powder and salt. Beat dry mixture gradually into butter mixture. Mix in liliko'i juice.

Pour into greased 9 x 5-inch loaf pan. Bake at 350°F for 55 to 60 minutes. Check for doneness with toothpick inserted in center. Do not over bake.

To make glaze, combine liliko'i juice with powdered sugar and stir until smooth. Serve cake slices drizzled with glaze.

Mahogany Chiffon Cake

Yield: 12 servings

8 eggs, separated
¾ cup boiling water
½ cup unsweetened cocoa
1¾ cups sifted cake flour
1¾ cups sugar, separated
1½ teaspoons baking soda
1 teaspoon salt
½ cup oil
2 teaspoons vanilla
½ teaspoon cream of tartar

Separate eggs first. Place whites in large mixing bowl and refrigerate until ready to use.

Combine boiling water and cocoa; set aside to cool.

In large mixing bowl, sift together flour, 1 cup of the sugar, baking soda and salt. Make a well and add oil, unbeaten egg yolks, cocoa mixture and vanilla. Beat until smooth. Set aside. Preheat oven 325°F.

Beat egg whites and cream of tartar until stiff. Gradually add remaining ¾ cup sugar. Pour cake mixture slowly over beaten egg whites, folding gently with a rubber scraper. Pour into ungreased 10-inch tube pan. Bake at 325°F for 65 to 70 minutes. Invert on funnel and hang until cooled. Slide knife around sides and center to release cake. Place cake on platter.

MOCHA FROSTING:

3 Tablespoons butter, softened
3 cups powdered sugar, sifted to remove lumps
5 Tablespoons unsweetened cocoa
1 Tablespoons instant coffee powder
5 Tablespoons evaporated milk
1 teaspoon vanilla

Beat together all ingredients and spread over cooled cake.

Mochi Muffins

Yield: 18 cupcakes

1 box mochiko (16 oz.)
1 cup sugar
½ teaspoon baking powder
3 eggs, beaten
1½ cups skimmed milk
¾ cup vegetable oil
1 can tsubushi an (18 oz.)

In large bowl, mix dry ingredients together. Add wet ingredients (except tsubushi an) and whisk together until blended and smooth. Place cupcake liners into muffin pans. Spray cupcake liners with Pam®.

Scoop tsubushi an into small bowl and stir to blend liquid with beans. Portion a little batter into cupcake containers (about half of total batter) and place about a heaping teaspoonful of tsubushian onto batter. Cover with remaining batter. Bake at 375°F for 30 to 35 minutes until light brown.

Cool in pans 10 minutes. Remove to wire racks. Cool completely.

> ✎ **NOTE:** *I bumped into Helen Kong one day in December 2000 and she told me about this unique muffin recipe which she got from her friend, Janet Kukino, a retired cafeteria manager from Ben Parker Elementary School. Since then Kathryn Kato, shared a similar recipe which originally came to her from Susan Yokouchi. I also found a similar recipe from See Dai Doo's 2010 newsletter reporting on their cooking demonstration.*
>
> ✎ **VARIATION:** *Janet Kukino said she substituted tsubushian with jellied cranberry sauce cut into little cubes and liked the result. The tops of the muffins should open up like a cross.*

Mae's Pineapple Upside-Down Cake

Yield: 24 servings

TOPPING:

4 Tablespoons butter
½ cup brown sugar
1 can crushed pineapple in pineapple juice, drained (20 oz.)
Cinnamon for sprinkling

On top of stove, using medium-low heat, melt butter in 9 x 13-inch pan. (Does not have to be completely melted.) Add brown sugar and mix together. Add crushed pineapple and mix together quickly so it does not carmalize. Sprinkle desired amount of cinnamon and mix together. Set aside to cool. Then start making cake.

CAKE:

1 cup butter (2 blocks), softened to room temperature
2 cups sugar
4 eggs, separated into yolks and whites
3 cups cake flour
4 teaspoons baking powder
Pinch salt
1 cup milk
1 teaspoon vanilla

In large bowl, beat together butter and sugar until creamy. Add 4 egg yolks to butter mixture; beat together and set aside. In small bowl, sift together cake flour, baking powder and salt (dry ingredients); set aside. In another small bowl, combine milk and vanilla (wet ingredients).

Mix in dry and wet ingredients, alternately, to butter mixture. Whip egg whites and fold into batter. Pour over crushed pineapple in pan. Bake at 350°F for 35 to 40 minutes, or longer until done. Check for doneness. Remove from oven and cool about 15 minutes. Use butter knife to loosen sides and flip cake over onto serving platter.

> ✎ NOTE: *This is not the usual pineapple upside-down cake. Mae Ushijima of Hilo likes this version that she originally got from Mrs. Albert Kami. It's made from "scratch" and it's worth it. Very delicious!*

Cakes & Breads

New York Style Cheesecake

Yield: 12 servings

15 graham crackers (30 squares), crushed
3 to 4 Tablespoons butter, melted

FILLING:

4 boxes cream cheese (8 oz.), softened
1½ cups sugar
¾ cup milk
4 eggs
1 cup sour cream
1 Tablespoon vanilla
¼ cup flour

CRUST:

In medium bowl, mix together crushed graham crackers with melted butter. Press onto bottom of greased 9-inch springform pan. Set aside.

FILLING:

In large bowl, beat cream cheese with sugar until smooth. Blend in milk and mix in eggs one at a time, mixing just enough to incorporate. Mix in sour cream, vanilla and flour until smooth. Pour into prepared crust.

Bake in preheated 350°F oven for 1 hour. Turn oven off and let cake cool in oven with door closed for 5 to 6 hours. (Prevents cake from cracking.) Refrigerate until serving.

NOTE: *Dr. Clayton Chong, my oncologist, is such a great cook! He was on a search for a cheesecake like the one he enjoyed in New York. After trying out many recipes, (he said one was so terrible he just dumped it) he found this to be the best so far. He's made this many times sharing with his family and friends. They all love it.*

Perfect Vanilla Cupcakes

Yield: 1 dozen cupcakes

¾ cup butter (1½ blocks), softened
1 cup sugar
1½ cups flour
1½ teaspoons baking powder
½ teaspoon salt
3 eggs
1 Tablespoon warm water
1 teaspoon vanilla extract

Beat butter and sugar until light and fluffy. In smaller bowl, combine flour, baking powder and salt; whisk together. Starting and ending with an egg, alternate adding eggs and flour to butter mixture, beating until well blended together. Beat in water and vanilla until just mixed. Pour into cupcake paper lined muffin pan. Bake at 400°F for 15 to 17 minutes or until cooked and golden. Remove from oven and let stand for a few minutes before turning them onto a wire rack to cool.

> ✍ **NOTE:** *Oven rack should be in the lower middle position. When cupcakes cool frost with your favorite frosting. See page 31 for cream cheese frosting or page 44 for chocolate frosting recipes.*
>
> ✍ **NOTE:** *Highly recommended by my daughter, Jennifer, who loves cupcakes.*

Cakes & Breads

Pineapple Banana Bread

Yield: 6 baby loaf pans

4 eggs
1 cup vegetable oil
2½ cups flour
1½ cups sugar
2 teaspoons baking powder
2 teaspoons baking soda
1 teaspoons salt
2 cups bananas (about 4 to 5 bananas), mashed
1 can crushed pineapple (8 oz.), drained
½ cup nuts (optional)

Grease 6 baby loaf pans (5¾ x 3¼ x 2-inches)*.

In large bowl, whisk eggs and add oil. Sift dry ingredients together and mix into egg mixture; blend well. Mix together mashed bananas and crushed pineapple. Add to mixture. Add nuts, if desired. Ladle equal amounts into pans. Bake at 350°F for 40 to 45 minutes. Check with toothpick inserted in center for doneness.

> **NOTE:** *At one of our '57 Hilo High class luncheons, Doris Tana-ka Niiyama made this and I really liked the taste. She said she was using my "Chocolate Banana Bread" recipe from* Hawai'i's Best Local Desserts *and discovered that she didn't have enough mashed bananas. So, being the creative person she is, she used crushed pineapple to make up the difference.*

*You may also use two 9 x 5-inch loaf pans. Bake at 350°F for 1 hour. Or three 8 x 3¾ x 2½-inch loaf pans. Bake at 350°F for 45 minutes. Doris used her small bundt pan.

Poppy Seed Bundt Cake with Icing

Yield: 12 servings

1 box yellow cake mix (15.25 oz.)
1 box instant Jell-O® vanilla pudding (3 oz.)
½ cup Wesson® vegetable oil
4 eggs
1 cup hot water
2 Tablespoons poppy seeds

Mix together cake mix and pudding; add oil then beat, adding eggs one at a time. Add hot water and poppy seeds; beat for 5 minutes. Pour into greased and floured bundt pan. Bake at 350°F for 35 to 40 minutes. Cool 15 minutes and loosen sides gently with butter knife. Invert over platter.

ICING:

1 cup sugar
¾ cup evaporated milk
½ cup butter (1 block)
1 teaspoon vanilla
½ cup nuts, chopped

Boil milk, butter and sugar for 5 minutes in small pot. Add vanilla and nuts. Drizzle desired amount of icing over warm cake. Serve remaining icing on the side for those who prefer more icing on their cake slices.

> 🖜 **NOTE:** *Icing is thin and doesn't quite harden but is delicious and adds to the cake.*

Pumpkin Date Cranberry Muffins

Yield: 24 muffins

1½ cups pumpkin
3 eggs
¾ cup Canola oil
¾ cup orange juice
1½ cups sugar

3 cups flour
1½ teaspoons baking soda
¾ teaspoon baking powder
¾ teaspoon each cinnamon, cloves, nutmeg, ginger

¾ cup dates, chopped and floured in 1 Tablespoon flour
   (use sieve to remove excess flour)
¾ cup walnuts, chopped
⅓ cup Craisins® (sweetened dried cranberries)

In large bowl, whisk eggs. Add pumpkin, oil, juice and sugar. Mix until blended.

Sift flour with baking soda, baking powder and spices. Add to pumpkin mixture and mix well.

Stir in dates, nuts and cranberries. Fill batter into 24 cupcake liners in muffin pans about ¾ full. Bake at 350°F for 20 to 22 minutes, or until toothpick inserted comes out clean.

> NOTE: *Irene Baba "tweaked" the original recipe and produced this tasty pumpkin muffin.*

Red Velvet Cupcake Surprise

Yield: 20 cupcakes

1 box German chocolate cake mix (18.25 oz.)
   (e.g. Betty Crocker® Super Moist with pudding in the mix)
1 box vanilla instant pudding (3.4 oz.)
1 cup sour cream
½ cup water
½ cup vegetable oil
1 bottle red food color (1 oz.)
3 eggs
1 cup miniature semisweet chocolate chips

Preheat oven to 350°F. Line cupcake cups with paper liners.

In large bowl, combine cake mix, instant pudding, sour cream, water, vegetable oil, food color and eggs. Blend on low for 30 seconds. Then beat on medium speed for 2 minutes, occasionally scraping sides of bowl. (Mixture will be thick.) Fold in chocolate chips. Spoon batter into each cupcake liner about ¾ full. Bake at 350°F for 20 to 22 minutes, or until done. Test with skewer or toothpick in center of cupcake. Cool thoroughly before frosting.

SUGGESTED CREAM CHEESE FROSTING FOR CUPCAKES:

1 box cream cheese (8 oz.), softened
½ cup butter (1 block), softened
2 to 3 cups powdered sugar, sifted (adjust to taste)
1 teaspoon vanilla

Blend cream cheese and butter in large mixing bowl with electric mixer on low speed, about 30 seconds. Add powdered sugar, a little at a time, with beater on low speed, about 1 minute. Add vanilla and beat on medium until fluffy, 1 minute more.

> 🖎 **NOTE:** *The mini chocolate chips give this a special taste! Thanks to Linda Shimamoto who shared this recipe with us.*

Siren Chocolate Cupcakes

Yield: 32 to 35 cupcakes

4 squares unsweetened chocolate (4 oz.),
  (e.g. Baker's® unsweetened baking chocolate squares)
½ cup butter (1 block)
2 eggs
2 cups buttermilk
2 teaspoons vanilla
2 ½ cups sifted cake flour
2 cups sugar
2 teaspoons baking soda

Melt butter and chocolate in saucepan on low heat.

In medium bowl, beat eggs until thick (about 2 minutes). Add buttermilk and vanilla; beat and set aside.

Sift cake flour, sugar and baking soda 3 times into large bowl. Pour egg mixture into dry ingredients and stir with spoon. Add melted butter and chocolate; stir with spoon until mixed well. Then beat with electric mixer 1 to 2 minutes. Pour into paper-lined cupcake pans, about ¾ full. Bake at 350°F for 15 minutes, or until done. When cool, frost with chocolate frosting. (See page 44)

✎ **NOTE:** *Catherine Thomas is often asked to make this delicious chocolate cake for family gatherings. "It is so easy," she says. She recommends using real vanilla extract, Darigold butter, Meadow gold buttermilk and Island eggs for best results. Do not overbeat chocolate and butter or it will get lumpy. "You want a smooth texture."*

✎ **VARIATION:** *Pour batter into 9 x 13-inch pan which has been greased, lined with waxed paper and greased lightly again. Or grease and flour pan. Bake at 350°F for 40 minutes, or until done.*

Chocolate Frosting

Yield: about 2½ cups

1 box powdered sugar (16 oz.)
½ cup evaporated milk
2 teaspoons vanilla
½ cup butter (1 block)
4 squares unsweetened chocolate (4 oz.)

Sift powdered sugar into medium bowl. Add evaporated milk and vanilla; mix together. Set aside.

Melt butter and chocolate square over low heat and add to powdered sugar mixture. Beat well. Frost cooled cake.

> 🥄 **NOTE:** *Catherine Thomas uses this frosting for her Siren Chocolate Cupcakes. (See page 43.) Need not be refrigerated.*

Two-Bite Easy Scones

Yield: 24 two-bite scones

1⅔ cups flour
¼ cup sugar
1½ teaspoons baking powder
½ teaspoon salt
½ cup cranberries, chopped
1 cup heavy cream (whipping cream)

Heat oven to 425°F. Mix all dry ingredients, including cranberries. Slowly add cream and mix. Spoon out onto lightly greased cookie sheet to make 24 small scones. Bake for 15 minutes.

> 🥄 **NOTE:** *Another tasty recipe from Gwen Amai Murai's collection of favorites.*

Sour Cream Cake

Yield: 24 servings

1 box Duncan Hines® Classic Yellow Cake Mix (16.5 oz.)
    or use any flavor
½ cup butter (1 block), melted and cooled
1 cup sour cream
4 eggs
½ cup oil
1 teaspoon vanilla

Lightly grease 9 x 13-inch pan.

Place all ingredients in large bowl. Beat at low speed until moistened (about 30 seconds). Beat at medium speed for 2 minutes. Pour into pan and bake at 325°F for 45 to 60 minutes. Cake is done when toothpick inserted in center comes out clean. Cool on wire rack at least 15 minutes before frosting. Frost with "Easy Frosting" below.

Easy Frosting

Yield: ¾ cup

½ cup whipping cream
1 cup semi-sweet chocolate chips
1 teaspoon vanilla

Heat whipping cream until just ready to boil. BUT DO NOT BOIL. Remove from heat; add chocolate chips and stir until chips are melted. Add vanilla. Pour over cooled cake.

✎ NOTE: *Cake is similar to a pound cake. It does need the frosting to add to the flavor. Refrigerate any left over cake. In fact, I liked it cold the next day.*

✎ SUGGESTION: *Use as hot fudge sauce or as a dip for strawberries.*

Sour Cream Chocolate Cupcakes

Yield: 24 cupcakes

DRY INGREDIENTS:

3 cups flour
2 cups sugar
½ cup Hershey's® Cocoa (natural unsweetened)
3 teaspoons baking soda
1 teaspoon salt

WET INGREDIENTS:

1 cup Wesson oil
2 eggs, beaten
2 teaspoons vanilla
1 cup sour cream (8 oz.)
1 cup boiling water

Sift together dry ingredients in large bowl. Add wet ingredients in order listed, Mix together thoroughly. Pour into 24 cupcake-lined baking cups. Bake at 350°F for 12 to 15 minutes.

> ✎ NOTE: *I used to make these easy chocolate cupcakes for my children many years ago after Pearl Ho brought some over for a luncheon. Somehow, over the years I misplaced the recipe card. I remembered how the children enjoyed them and I wanted to include it in this dessert book. Thanks to Pearl who took the time to locate her recipe for me.*

Triple Chocolate Cake

Yield: 24 to 30 servings

1 box chocolate cake or Devil's Food cake mix (18.25 oz.)
1 box instant chocolate pudding mix (3 oz.)
½ cup water
½ cup oil
4 eggs
1 container sour cream (8 oz.)
3 to 4 teaspoons instant coffee
1 bag mini chocolate morsels (12 oz.) or less

Beat all ingredients together (except chocolate chips) with mixer until smooth. Stir in chocolate chips. Pour into greased 9 x 13-inch pan. Bake at 350°F for 45 minutes. Cool completely. Sprinkle with powdered sugar, if desired, or frost with your favorite frosting.

> **NOTE:** *At a potluck luncheon at Mutsumi Pang's home we were served this triple chocolate cake, one of many desserts offered that day. Mutsumi had baked this very easy and tasty cake which we enjoyed. She said she found this recipe in a Hilo cookbook put together many years ago by the Church of the Holy Cross. She added her little touch by mixing in instant coffee.*

Plum-Good Prune Cake

Yield: about 20 servings

1 package pitted prunes (9 oz.; about 27 prunes)
2 Tablespoons bourbon or sherry

3 cups flour
2 teaspoons baking soda
1 teaspoon salt
1 teaspoon cinnamon
½ teaspoon cloves

1½ cups salad oil
2 cups sugar
3 eggs
2 cups apples, coarsely shredded (about 2 to 3 apples)
1 cup nuts, chopped
Powdered sugar, for sprinkling

Coarsely chop prunes; sprinkle with liquor, mix together and let stand several hours or overnight. Grease and flour bundt pan; set aside.

Sift flour with baking soda, salt and spices. In larger bowl, beat oil with sugar and eggs for 2 minutes at medium speed. Gradually mix in dry ingredients at low speed. Mix in prunes, apples and nuts. Pour in bundt pan. Bake at 325°F for 1½ hours. Cool in pan for 15 minutes. Invert onto cooling rack to cool completely. Sprinkle with powdered sugar.

> 🍮 **NOTE:** *Highly recommended by Katherine Kato as one of her family favorites. Don't let the word "prune" scare you. Try it. You might like it.*

T.J.'s Sour Cream Coffee Cake

Yield: 24 servings

DRY INGREDIENTS:

2 cups flour
1 teaspoon baking powder
1 teaspoon baking soda
½ teaspoon salt

TOPPING:

3 Tablespoons brown sugar
½ cup nuts, chopped
1 teaspoon cinnamon

WET INGREDIENTS:

1 cup butter (2 blocks)
1 cup sugar
2 eggs
1 teaspoon vanilla
1 cup sour cream

In small bowl, mix together flour, baking powder, baking soda and salt. Set aside.

In smaller bowl, mix together topping ingredients; set aside.

In large bowl, beat butter and sugar until light and fluffy. Add eggs and beat. Add vanilla and sour cream; beat together. Add dry ingredients to butter mixture and mix together. Spread half of the batter into greased 9 x 13-inch pan. Sprinkle half of the topping mixture evenly over batter. Add remaining batter and top with remaining topping. Bake at 350°F for 30 to 35 minutes.

> ✎ NOTE: *T.J., Ruby Saito's grandson says, "Yummy, just out of the oven."*

Walnut Coconut Bundt Cake

Yield: 12 Servings

2 cups sugar
1 cup buttermilk
1 cup canola oil
4 eggs
2 teaspoons coconut extract
3 cups flour
½ teaspoon baking powder
½ teaspoon baking soda
½ teaspoon salt
1 cup flaked coconut
1 cup walnuts, chopped

SYRUP:

1 cup sugar
½ cup water
2 Tablespoons butter
1 teaspoon coconut extract

In large bowl, beat sugar, buttermilk, oil, eggs and extract until well blended. In smaller bowl, combine flour, baking powder, baking soda and salt; gradually beat into sugar mixture until blended. Stir in coconut and walnuts.

Pour batter into greased and floured Bundt pan. Bake at 325°F for 60 to 70 minutes or until toothpick inserted near center comes out clean. Cool for 10 minutes.

In small saucepan, bring sugar and water to a boil over medium heat. Cook and stir for 5 minutes or until mixture is slightly reduced. Remove from heat; stir in butter and coconut extract.

Remove cake by sliding butter knife along sides to loosen. Turn upside down onto wire rack. Poke holes in warm cake with a skewer and slowly pour syrup over cake. Cool completely. Carefully transfer cake to platter.

✎ **NOTE:** *Texture is more like a bread. Not too sweet and very tasty.*

Pies

Avocado Chiffon Pie

Yield: 8 servings

1 (9-inch) pie crust, baked

3 eggs, separated (whites in refrigerator)
¾ cup sugar, separated
1½ Tablespoons butter
1 envelope Knox® gelatin
¼ cup water
1 cup avocado, mashed
Cool Whip® for topping (about half of 8 oz. container)

In saucepan, cook egg yolks, ¼ cup of the sugar and butter on medium low, stirring constantly, until slightly thick (about 5 minutes). Remove from heat. Dissolve gelatin in water; stir into hot mixture until blended. Transfer to large mixing bowl.

When mixture is slightly cooled, stir in avocado. Set aside.

In medium bowl, beat egg whites until soft peaks form. Add remaining ½ cup sugar gradually. Continue beating until stiff. Fold gently into avocado mixture. Pour into pie shell. Chill and top with Cool Whip®.

> ▦ NOTE: *This recipe is definitely for avocado lovers. Ruby Saito's Aunty Elaine Komo from Kona shared this great recipe.*
>
> ▦ TIPS: *Ruby used the "Easy Pie Crust" recipe on page 65 and she said that works well with this pie. I used "Aunty Sarah's Pie Pastry" recipe on page 53 and that worked well, too.*

Aunty Sarah's Pie Pastry

Yield: 1 pie crust

1½ cups flour
2 teaspoons sugar
½ teaspoon salt
½ cup Crisco®, cold
3 to 4 Tablespoons cold water

Sift together flour, sugar and salt. Cut Crisco® into dry ingredients. Add cold water, a tablespoon at a time. Gently toss with fork and knead gently to form a round ball. Let rest for ½ hour.

Place ball on waxed paper over a floured board and flatten ball slightly. Cover ball with another waxed paper and roll between the two pieces of waxed paper. Carefully remove rolled out dough and place in pan; flute edges. Prick bottom and sides well with fork. (Do not prick pastry if filling and crust are to be baked together.) Bake at 425°F for 15 to 20 minutes or until brown. Watch to see that crust does not burn.

> ☙ NOTE: *Thanks to Agnes Leong who shared Aunty Sarah's pie pastry.*
>
> ☙ TIPS: *Always roll spoke-fashion, going from center to edge of dough using light strokes. If edges split, pinch together.*

Avocado
Cream Cheese Squares

Yield: 24 servings

CRUST:

1½ cups flour
¼ cup powdered sugar
1 cup butter (2 blocks)
½ cup nuts, chopped

Whisk flour and sugar. Cut in butter until well blended. Add nuts. Press into greased 9 x 13-inch pan. Bake at 350°F for 20 minutes or until golden brown. Cool.

MIDDLE LAYER:

1 box lemon Jell-O® (3 oz.)
1 cup boiling water
1 package gelatin dissolved in ¼ cup water
1 box cream cheese (8 oz.)
½ cup powdered sugar
1 cup Cool Whip®

In small saucepan boil water and mix in Jell-O® until dissolved; add gelatin dissolved in ¼ cup water. Set aside to cool.

In 2 quart bowl, beat together cream cheese and sugar. Add Jell-O® mixture; blend well. Add Cool Whip®; mix to blend. Pour into cooled crust; refrigerate until firm (at least one hour).

TOP LAYER:

1 large box lime Jell-O® (6 oz.)
½ cup sugar
2 cups boiling water
1 package gelatin dissolved in ¼ cup water
1 cup ripe avocado, mashed
½ cup milk or cream
½ cup mayonnaise
Cool Whip®

Dissolve Jell-O® and sugar in 2 cups boiling water; add dissolved gelatin. Cool.

In large bowl, add avocado, milk and mayonnaise; beat with mixer until well blended. Add Jell-O® mixture. Pour over cooled and hardened cream cheese layer. Chill to set. Top with desired amount of Cool Whip®.

> ✎ NOTE: *Ruby Saito refined this recipe over a period of 2 years whenever she had a batch of avocados. I and many of her friends taste-tested the different versions and we're selecting this delicious version for this cookbook.*
>
> ✎ SUGGESTION: *Avocados can be mashed and frozen in 1 cup portions. Ruby used Ziploc® snack bags for easy usage.*

Banana Pie

Yield: 8 servings

3 to 4 cups apple bananas (ripe but firm), cut into ¼-inch slices
1 cup pineapple juice

½ cup sugar
3 Tablespoons flour
1 teaspoon cinnamon
½ teaspoon nutmeg
Pinch salt

1 Tablespoon butter
2 Tablespoons milk

Soak sliced bananas in pineapple juice 20 to 30 minutes.

"EASY PIE CRUST" (MAKE 2):

1½ cups flour
½ teaspoon salt
1½ teaspoons sugar
½ cup oil
2 Tablespoons milk

While bananas are soaking, prepare bottom crust. Sift together flour, salt and sugar into ungreased 9-inch pie pan. Whip oil and milk with fork until cloudy; pour over flour mixture. Mix with fork until blended. Press dough into pie pan. Set aside.

In mixing bowl, prepare another "Easy Pie Crust" for top crust. Set aside.

Preheat oven to 400°F.

Drain bananas, reserving juice for another use. Combine sugar, flour, cinnamon, nutmeg and salt; mix with bananas. Pour filling into prepared pie pan. Crumble second "Easy Pie Crust" evenly over banana filling. Dot with butter and dab lightly with milk. Bake for 30 to 35 minutes. Serve warm or cold.

> ✎ **SUGGESTION:** *Mix together 1 teaspoon sugar and ¼ teaspoon cinnamon; sprinkle over top crust before baking for added flavor.*
>
> ✎ **NOTE:** *Very delicious! I received a banana pie recipe from Wendy Calizar and also one from Ruby Saito who got it from Pam Honbo. Ruby used the "Easy Pie crust" recipe which eliminated rolling out pie crusts which makes the pie much easier to prepare.*
>
> ✎ *Another option is to use Marie Callender's® frozen 2 Deep Dish Pie Shells. Follow baking directions. This is the easiest of all.*

Crumb Crust

Yield: Crust for 1 (9-inch) pie pan

1¼ cups fine crumbs (e.g. graham crackers, about 14 rectangle pieces)
3 Tablespoons sugar
⅓ cup butter, melted

Combine ingredients and mix well. Press firmly over bottom and sides of 9-inch pie pan or bottom of 8-inch square pan. Chill for 1 hour or bake at 375°F for 8 minutes. Cool before filling. Fill with ice cream, chiffon or cream fillings.

> ✎ **NOTE:** *For 8-inch pie pan, reduce crumbs to 1 cup and sugar to 2 Tablespoons.*
>
> ✎ **SUGGESTION:** *Substitute graham cracker crumbs with chocolate wafers or gingersnaps.*

Pear Dessert

Yield: 24 servings

CRUST:

1 cup butter (2 blocks), softened
2 Tablespoons sugar
1½ cups flour
1 cup macadamia nuts, finely chopped

Beat butter and sugar until light and fluffy. Add flour and mix with heavy spoon; mix in nuts. Spread and press in bottom of 9 x 13-inch pan. Bake at 350°F for 20 minutes or till golden brown. Remove from oven and set aside to cool.

FILLING:

2 boxes cream cheese (8 oz. each), softened
½ cup sugar
1 teaspoon vanilla
2 eggs

Beat together cream cheese and sugar and vanilla. Add eggs; beat together to blend thoroughly. Spread over cooled crust.

TOPPING:

3 cans sliced pears (15.25 oz. each), drained
1 teaspoon cinnamon

Slice slightly thicker pear pieces and place pear slices evenly on cream cheese filling. Sprinkle cinnamon on top. Bake at 375°F for 25 to 30 minutes. Cut while warm. Cool and refrigerate.

Blueberry Cream Cheese Pie

Yield: 24 servings

CRUST:

1½ cups flour
¼ cup brown sugar
1 cup butter (2 blocks)
½ cup nuts, chopped

Mix together flour and brown sugar. Cut in butter. Mix in nuts. Press into 9 x 13-inch pan. Bake at 350°F for 15 to 20 minutes or until golden brown. Remove from oven. Cool.

FILLING:

1 cup whipping cream (e.g. Meadow Gold® Whipping Cream)
1 box cream cheese (8 oz.), softened
¾ cup powdered sugar, sifted
1 teaspoon vanilla
1 can blueberry pie filling (21 oz.)

Beat whipping cream until peaks form; set aside.

In large bowl beat together cream cheese, sugar and vanilla. Fold whipped cream into cream cheese mixture; spread over crust. Top with blueberry pie filling. Chill for 2 hours or longer before serving.

> NOTE: *Okay, Cheryl, this is for you. You requested Grandma Watanabe's blueberry recipe and here it is. It has less cream cheese and uses fresh whipping cream instead of Cool Whip®. Grandma's original recipe called for Avoset® whipping cream which is no longer on the shelves.*

Chocolate Haupia Pie

Yield: 24 servings

CRUST:

- 1 cup butter (2 blocks), chilled
- 2 cups flour
- 4 Tablespoons sugar
- ½ cup nuts, chopped

FILLING:

- 3 cans coconut milk (13.5 oz. each)
- 1¼ cups water
- 2 cups sugar
- ½ cup Nestlé® cooking cocoa
- 13 Tablespoons cornstarch
- ¼ teaspoon salt
- 1 Tablespoon coconut extract

Cut butter into flour and sugar; add nuts and press into 9 x 13-inch pan. Bake at 350°F for 30 minutes. Set aside to cool.

Combine coconut milk and water in pot. Cook on medium heat until small bubbles appear around sides of pot. Stir often to avoid burning. Add sugar, cocoa, cornstarch and salt. Stir constantly until mixture starts to bubble and cook about 8 minutes more, stirring and scraping sides constantly. Remove from stove and add coconut extract. Pour over crust. Cool about 5 to 10 minutes and cover with waxed paper directly on mixture to avoid cracks. Refrigerate until firm.

> ✎ NOTE: *Delicious! This is a favorite party dessert. If desired, add a squirt of whipped cream over each serving.*

Custard Pie

Yield: 8 servings

4 eggs, slightly beaten
½ cup sugar
¼ teaspoon salt
1 teaspoon vanilla
2½ cups milk, scalded
1 (9-inch) pie shell, unbaked
Dash nutmeg

Preheat oven to 475°F. Thoroughly mix together eggs, sugar, salt and vanilla. Slowly add scalded milk to mixture, mixing to blend. Place unbaked pie shell on baking sheet on middle rack. Slowly pour mixture into pie shell. Sprinkle nutmeg over. Bake at 475°F for 5 minutes. Reduce heat to 425°F and bake 10 minutes longer or until knife inserted about halfway comes out cleanly. (Check middle and side.)

> ✎ NOTE: *When Jennie Tyau's grandson was about 12 years old, he learned how to make this easy custard pie from Jennie. He was able to memorize the ingredients and would bake it often. Jennie gave me this recipe after my cooking demo at a meeting of the O'ahu Retired Teachers' Association.*

Cream Cheese Pumpkin Pie

Yield: 24 servings

CRUST:

¾ cup butter (1½ blocks), softened
¼ cup brown sugar
1½ cups flour
½ cup nuts, chopped

Beat butter and brown sugar; add flour and blend. Mix in nuts.

Spread evenly in 9 x 13-inch pan. Partially bake at 350°F for about 7 to 10 minutes. Remove; set aside.

CREAM CHEESE LAYER:

2 boxes cream cheese (8 oz. each), softened
½ cup sugar
1 teaspoon vanilla
2 eggs

Beat cream cheese; add sugar and beat together. Add vanilla and eggs. Mix well. Spread evenly over partially baked crust.

FILLING:

4 eggs, slightly beaten
1 can pumpkin (29 oz.)
1½ cups sugar
1 teaspoon salt
1 teaspoon cinnamon
¼ teaspoon ginger
¼ teaspoon nutmeg
2 cans evaporated milk (12 oz. each)

Increase oven temperature to 425°F. Mix all filling ingredients; carefully ladle over cream cheese mixture, partially filling pan. Carefully place in oven and add more pumpkin filling. Extra pumpkin filling may be poured into custard dishes and baked along with pie. Bake at 425°F for 15 minutes, then at 350°F for 45 to 55 minutes. Insert knife to test for doneness. Refrigerate when cool.

SUGGESTION: *Top with Cool Whip® when serving.*

NOTE: *This is an old favorite recipe shared by Juliet Morita who taught at Puohala Elementary in the 70s. We all love it.*

Crispy Apricot Turnovers

Yield: 6 servings

6 sheets phyllo (or whole-wheat phyllo)
Butter-flavored cooking oil spray
¾ cup Smucker's® Simply Fruit apricot jam

Thaw phyllo (see directions on box). Preheat oven 400°F.

Peel off and lay one phyllo sheet down on a cookie sheet (your working surface.). With narrow end toward you spray with cooking spray. Fold sheet in thirds lengthwise. Spray again. Spoon 2 tablespoons fruit jam about 1½ inches from the bottom edge. Fold the lower left-hand corner of phyllo diagonally to right side, covering the filling. Continue folding in flag-style until the end of the sheet. Spray both sides of the turnover and lay on baking sheet. Repeat the process. Bake for 15 minutes or until golden brown. Serve warm.

NOTE: *Place any leftover in sealed container. Need not be refrigerated. Can be reheated in oven or toaster oven but not necessary. My husband, Don, and our Popo liked it a lot. I actually liked it better the next day without reheating. It was still crispy.*

Deep-Dish Apple Pie

Yield: one 10-inch pie

PIE CRUST:

3 cups flour
1 teaspoon salt
1 Tablespoon sugar
¾ cup unsalted butter (1½ blocks), very cold
⅓ cup Crisco®, very cold
6 to 8 Tablespoons ice water

In large bowl, sift together flour, salt and sugar. Cut cold butter and cold Crisco® into flour mixture until size of peas. Add ice water, beginning with 2 Tablespoons and mix gently. Knead gently and form a ball. Dump out on floured board and roll into a ball. Wrap in plastic wrap and refrigerate 30 minutes.

FILLING:

4 pounds Granny Smith apples, peeled, quartered and cored
Zest of 1 lemon
Zest of 1 orange
2 Tablespoons lemon juice
1 Tablespoon orange juice
½ cup sugar, plus 1 teaspoon for sprinkling
¼ cup flour
1 teaspoon salt
¼ teaspoon cinnamon
½ teaspoon nutmeg
⅛ teaspoon allspice
1 egg, beaten with 1 Tablespoon water for egg wash

In large bowl, combine zests, juices, sugar, flour, salt, cinnamon, nutmeg and allspice. Cut each apple quarter in thirds crosswise; place in bowl with spices and toss gently to coat. Set aside.

Cut cold dough in half. Roll each piece on well-floured board into a circle, rolling from center to edge, turning and flouring the dough so it doesn't stick to the board. Fold dough in half and drape over pie pan extending ½ inch over rim. Trim off excess. (Do not stretch dough. If too small, reroll again.)

Place apple filling in pie pan. Brush the edge of crust with egg wash so top crust will adhere. Top with second crust and trim edge to about 1 inch over the rim. Tuck the edge of the top crust under the edge of the bottom crust and crimp the two together with a fork or with fingers. Brush the entire top crust with the egg wash, sprinkle with 1 teaspoon sugar and cut five slits on top.

Place pie on baking sheet and bake at 400°F for 1 to 1½ hours, or until crust is browned and juices begin to bubble out.

> 🥧 NOTE: *Recipe calls for a 10-inch pie pan. I use my 9-inch pan and adjust baking time. Do not over bake else apples will turn into applesauce.*

Easy Pie Crust

Yield: one 9-inch pie crust

1½ cups flour
1½ teaspoons sugar
1 teaspoon salt
½ cup oil
2 Tablespoons cold milk

Sift together flour, sugar and salt into ungreased 9-inch pie pan. Whip oil and milk with fork until cloudy; pour over flour mixture. Mix with fork until blended. Press dough into pie pan.

> 🥧 NOTE: *For baked pie shell, prick here and there. Bake at 400°F for 10 to 15 minutes until light brown.*

Fruit Tart

Yield: 6 to 8 servings

1 (9-inch) pie shell, baked; or Keebler® Graham Ready Crust

GLAZE:

2 teaspoons sugar
1 teaspoon cornstarch
½ cup orange juice

Combine sugar and cornstarch in small saucepan; stir in orange juice. Cook on medium heat until thickened and bubbly, stirring constantly. Remove from heat; cool.

FILLING:

1 kiwi fruit, peeled and sliced
¾ cup bananas, thinly sliced
1 to 2 cups strawberries, hulled and thinly sliced

Arrange kiwi in center of pie crust, bananas around kiwi and strawberries around bananas. Spoon glaze over fruit. Chill for 1 hour.

Guava Delight

Yield: 24 to 30 servings

CRUST:

1 cup butter (2 blocks), softened
¼ cup powdered sugar (or brown sugar)
1½ cups flour

Beat butter and sugar until light and fluffy. Add flour; mix together. Press into 9 x 13-inch pan. Bake at 350°F for 15 to 20 minutes or until brown. Cool.

FILLING:

2 boxes cream cheese (8 oz. each), softened
1½ cups powdered sugar
4 Tablespoons frozen guava juice, thawed
1 container Cool Whip® (8 oz.)

Beat cream cheese. Mix in powdered sugar. Add guava juice. Fold in Cool Whip®; spread over crust. Refrigerate.

TOPPING:

1 can frozen guava juice (12 oz.), thawed, less 4 Tablespoons used in filling
2 Tablespoons cornstarch
½ cup water

Boil guava juice. Combine cornstarch and water; stir into guava juice. Stir until thick and clear. Remove from heat and cool. Spread over cream cheese; refrigerate.

> ✎ **NOTE:** *Pie is tasty although a little tart. Recipe shared by Ruby Saito and Kelly Goodin.*

Jell-O® Cream Cheese Pie

Yield: 24 servings

CRUST:

> 1½ cups flour
> ¼ cup brown sugar
> ¾ cup butter (1½ blocks), cold
> ½ cup nuts, chopped

Mix flour and sugar; cut in butter until crumbly. Mix in nuts. Press dough into 9 x 13-inch pan. Bake at 375°F for 10 minutes or until the top browns.

FILLING:

> 1 box lemon Jell-O® (3 oz.)
> 1 cup hot water
> 1 box cream cheese (8 oz.), softened
> ½ cup sugar
> 1 cup whipping cream (½ pint) e.g. Meadow Gold® Whipping Cream

Dissolve lemon Jell-O® in hot water; set aside to cool. In large bowl, beat cream cheese and sugar together. In medium bowl, whip whipping cream and add to cream cheese mixture; blend. Add cooled Jell-O®; blend and pour over cooled crust. Chill until firm (preferably overnight).

TOPPING:

> 2 boxes Jell-O® (3 oz. each), any desired flavor
> 3 cups hot water

Dissolve Jell-O® in hot water. Cool. Pour over cream cheese mixture, slowly and carefully. Chill until firm before serving.

Lemon Chiffon Pie

Yield: 24 servings

CRUST:

¾ cup butter (1½ blocks), softened
2 Tablespoons powdered sugar
1½ cups flour
¾ cup nuts, chopped

Beat butter and sugar until light and fluffy; add flour and mix with wooden spoon until blended. Mix in nuts. Press into 9 x 13-inch pan. Bake at 425°F for 10 minutes or until golden brown. Cool.

FILLING:

8 egg yolks, beaten
1 cup sugar
1 cup lemon juice (about 3 large juicy lemons)
1 teaspoon salt
1 cup water
2 envelopes unflavored gelatin
2 Tablespoons grated lemon peel

Combine egg yolks, sugar, lemon juice and salt in double boiler and cook on low heat, stirring constantly, until thick. Remove from heat and beat on low speed to blend. Blend gelatin with 1 cup water and add to mixture; stir until gelatin dissolves. Add lemon peel and cool in refrigerator until partially set (30 to 45 minutes).

TOPPING:

8 egg whites
1 cup sugar
1 cup whipped cream

Beat egg whites until stiff. Then gradually beat in sugar. Fold into cooled mixture. Pour into prepared crust. Chill until firm. Top with whipped cream.

> ✎ NOTE: *During lemon season when there is an abundance of fruit, this is a great dessert to make. Be sure to grate lemons before squeezing.*

Lemon Delight

Yield: 24 servings

CRUST:

> ¾ cup butter (1½ blocks)
> 1½ cups flour
> ½ cup nuts, chopped

Cut butter into flour until crumbly. Add nuts. Press into greased 9 x 13-inch pan. Bake at 350°F for 25 minutes, or until brown. Cool.

FIRST LAYER:

> 1 box cream cheese (8 oz.), softened
> ½ cup powdered sugar
> ½ container Cool Whip® (half of 12 oz. container)

Beat together cream cheese and powdered sugar. Blend in Cool Whip®. Spread over crust. Place in refrigerator to chill 10 minutes.

SECOND LAYER:

> 2 boxes instant lemon pudding (3 oz. each)
> 3 cups milk

Mix together and spread over cream cheese layer. Chill 10 minutes.

TOPPING:

Spread the other half of Cool Whip® over. Refrigerate to set before serving.

Lemon Pie in Meringue Shell

Yield: 6 to 8 servings

3 egg whites
¼ teaspoon cream of tartar
1½ cups sugar, divided

4 egg yolks
3 Tablespoons lemon juice
1 Tablespoon grated lemon peel
⅛ teaspoon salt
2 cups heavy whipping cream

Place egg whites in small bowl; let stand at room temperature for 30 minutes. Add cream of tartar; beat until soft peaks form. Gradually add 1 cup of the sugar, 1 Tablespoon at a time, beating until stiff peaks form. Spread onto bottom and up the sides of a greased 9-inch pie plate. Bake at 350°F for 25 to 30 minutes. Cool on wire rack.

In large saucepan, combine egg yolks, lemon juice, lemon peel, salt and remaining ½ cup sugar. Cook and stir over medium heat until mixture reaches 160°F or is thick enough to coat the back of a metal spoon. Reduce heat and cook and stir 2 minutes longer. Remove from heat. Cool to room temperature without stirring.

In medium bowl, beat whipping cream. Fold half of the whipped cream into lemon filling. Spread into meringue shell. Top with remaining whipped cream. Refrigerate overnight before serving.

> ✎ **NOTE:** *Jeri Barnes absolutely loves this pie! Her friend brought this pie over and after tasting it she requested her friend bake it again. She shared the recipe with me with the stipulation that I bake it and invite her over for coffee.*

Liliko'i Chiffon Pie

Yield: one 9-inch pie

1 (9-inch) pie shell, baked

1 cup sugar, separated
1 envelope Knox® gelatin
Pinch salt
4 eggs, separated (yolks at room temperature, whites in
    refrigerator)
¼ cup water
½ cup fresh liliko'i juice
Cool Whip® for garnish or topping (about half of 8 oz. container)

Mix together ½ cup of the sugar, gelatin and salt; set aside.

In medium bowl, beat egg yolks until light and slightly frothy. Add water and liliko'i juice to yolks; beat. Add sugar and gelatin mixture; mix together. Transfer to saucepan and cook over medium heat, stirring constantly, until thick and bubbles begin to appear. Set aside to cool.

Beat egg whites on high until soft peaks form. Add remaining ½ cup sugar gradually. Continue beating until stiff. Fold gently into liliko'i mixture. Pour into pie shell. Chill and top with Cool Whip®.

> ✎ **NOTE:** *Ruby Saito, who shared this recipe, said, "Many years ago, I got this recipe from my friend, Joyce Hayashi. She learned to make this pie growing up on Kaua'i. Whenever I am able to get fresh liliko'i juice, I use this recipe. It never fails."*

Magic Crust Custard Pie

Yield: 8 servings

¼ cup butter, softened
¾ cup sugar
4 eggs
2 cups milk (2%)
½ cup flour
2 teaspoons vanilla
Pinch salt
Nutmeg for sprinkling

Preheat oven 350°F. Butter a 9-inch, deep dish pie pan; set aside.

Beat together butter, sugar and eggs until just blended. Add milk, flour, vanilla and salt; blend. Place pie pan on oven shelf. Carefully pour custard filling into pie pan. Sprinkle with nutmeg. Bake for 45 minutes.

> ✎ NOTE: *The flour will settle to make its own crust. Delicious! Best served warm. Pie and recipe were shared by Kelly Goodin who enjoys baking and often shares her treats with my family.*
>
> ✎ SUGGESTION FOR A QUICK AND EASY PREPARATION: *Kelly put all the ingredients (except for nutmeg) into a blender. Blend for 30 seconds. Pour custard filling into pie pan. Continue with above directions.*

Little Coconut Pies

Yield: 32 pieces

COCONUT FILLING:

2 cups sugar
½ cup corn starch
3 cups water
6½ cups coconut flakes (2½ [7 oz.] packages)

In saucepan, combine sugar and corn starch. Gradually mix in water. Cook on medium heat, first stirring occasionally, then constantly as mixture heats up. Reduce heat to low when mixture begins to boil. Continue cooking and stirring on low until mixture thickens. Mix in coconut flakes in small batches and continue to cook and stir for few more minutes. Remove from heat; set aside to cool.

CRUST:

4½ cups flour
½ teaspoon salt
2 cups Imperial® margarine (4 blocks), softened to room
   temperature
8 to 10 Tablespoons ice water
2 Tablespoons cream

Sift flour and salt together. Cut in margarine until mixture resembles cornmeal. Add ice water a little at a time to moisten mixture. (Begin with 2 Tablespoons ice water.) Knead lightly, press together and form into a ball. Divide into fourths. Tear 8 pieces from each fourth. Roll or flatten each piece and fill half with heaping Tablespoonful of coconut filling. Fold and mold around coconut mix to form a "half-moon" pie. Crimp edges together. Brush with cream. Bake on ungreased cookie sheet at 375°F for 25 to 30 minutes. (Check after 20 minutes.)

> ✎ NOTE: *Joyce Takahashi from Hilo shared this when I started talking about the small Mom and Pop stores in Hilo a long time ago which sold these half-moon shaped little pies. They were also filled with apple pie filling or lima bean an.*

Macadamia Nut Cream Pie

Yield: 6 servings

1 (9-inch) pie shell, baked

FILLING:

3 Tablespoons cornstarch
½ cup sugar
¼ teaspoon salt
¼ cup macadamia nuts, chopped
4 egg yolks, slightly beaten
2 cups milk, scalded
1 Tablespoon butter
½ teaspoon vanilla
1 container Cool Whip® (8 oz.)
¼ cup macadamia nuts, chopped

Combine cornstarch, sugar, salt and macadamia nuts in top of double boiler; add egg yolks, stirring until well blended. Place over bottom part of double boiler with water steaming at low-medium heat. Stir in milk slowly and cook, stirring constantly until mixture thickens. Add butter and vanilla; mix. Remove from heat and cool thoroughly. Pour into baked pie crust. Chill until set. Spread desired amount of Cool Whip® and sprinkle macadamia nuts over.

> 🖎 NOTE: *Recipe shared by Gladys Aloiau who taught kindergarten at ʻAikahi Elementary with me. Everything she baked was so delicious.*

Mandarin Cream Pie

Yield: 24 servings

CRUST:

1 cup butter (2 blocks), softened
2 Tablespoons powdered sugar
1½ cups flour
½ cup nuts, chopped

Beat together butter and sugar. Add flour; mix with wooden spoon. Add nuts. Press into 9 x 13-inch pan. Bake at 350°F for 16 to 20 minutes or until light brown. Cool.

FILLING:

2 cans mandarin oranges (11 oz. each), drained (reserve juice)
½ cup mandarin juice
1 Tablespoon sugar
1 container sour cream (8 oz.)
1 cup whole milk (or slightly less)
2 boxes instant vanilla pudding (3.4 oz. each)
1 container Cool Whip® (8 oz.)
Chopped nuts for sprinkling

Combine mandarin juice, sugar, sour cream, milk and pudding. Fold in mandarin oranges. Pour into cooled crust. Top with Cool Whip® and sprinkle with nuts. Refrigerate at least 2 hours before serving.

> 🍰 NOTE: *When I shared this dessert at a recent potluck everyone liked it but some mentioned that the filling was a little soft. So I added the choice of using slightly less whole milk.*

Orange Cream Dessert

Yield: 24 servings

CRUST:

¾ cups butter (1½ blocks)
¼ cup brown sugar
1½ cups flour
½ cup nuts, chopped

Beat butter and sugar. Add flour and nuts; mix well. Spread into 9 x 13-inch pan. Bake at 375°F for 10 minutes or until golden brown. Cool.

FILLING:

1 box cream cheese (8 oz.), softened
¾ cup sugar
4 ounces Cool Whip® (half of a 8 oz. container)

Beat cream cheese and sugar. Fold in Cool Whip®. Spread filling evenly on crust. Chill 30 minutes.

TOPPING:

1 envelope unflavored Knox® gelatin
1 cup water, divided
1 package orange Jell-O® (6 oz.)
2 cups hot water
2 cups orange sherbet, remove from freezer to begin thawing
2 cans mandarin oranges (11 oz. each), drained

Soften unflavored gelatin in ¼ cup of the water; set aside. In large bowl, dissolve Jell-O® with 2 cups hot water; add softened gelatin and remaining ¾ cup water. Stir until dissolved. Stir in Mandarin oranges and sherbet. Ladle mixture over cream cheese filling. Refrigerate.

✎ NOTE: *Very light and refreshing taste.*

Pecan Pie

Yield: 6 to 8 servings

1 (9-inch) pie crust, unbaked

1 cup light corn syrup
1 cup dark brown sugar, firmly packed
3 eggs, slightly beaten
$\frac{1}{3}$ cup butter, melted
$\frac{1}{2}$ teaspoon salt
1 teaspoon vanilla
1¼ cups pecan halves

In large bowl, combine corn syrup, sugar, eggs, butter, salt and vanilla; mix well. Pour into unbaked pie crust; sprinkle pecans evenly over. Bake at 350°F for 50 to 60 minutes or until center is set (may take more time). Insert toothpick in center to check for doneness. Cool.

> NOTE: *If pie appears to be getting too brown, cover with foil for the remaining baking time. This pie is delicious! Very rich but great for the Christmas holidays.*

Pies

Shortbread Pumpkin Squares

Yield: 24 servings

CRUST:

2 cups flour
¼ cup sugar
1 cup butter (2 blocks)

Sift flour and sugar together. Cut in cold butter until crumbly. Press into 9 x 13-inch pan. Bake at 375°F for 20 minutes or until golden brown.

Set aside to cool (about 15 to 20 minutes).

FILLING:

4 eggs, slightly beaten
1 can pumpkin (29 oz.) or 3 cups
1½ cups sugar
1 teaspoon salt
1 teaspoon cinnamon
1 teaspoon nutmeg
½ teaspoon pumpkin spice
2 cans evaporated milk (12 oz. each)

Mix filling ingredients and pour over cooled baked crust. Bake at 350°F for 1 hour 10 minutes or until knife comes out cleanly in the center.

Cookies
& Bars

Gingersnap Cookies

Yield: 150 cookies

4½ cups flour
½ teaspoon salt
2½ teaspoons baking soda
2 teaspoons ginger
1½ teaspoons cinnamon
1½ teaspoons cloves

1½ cups Crisco® shortening
1½ cups sugar
2 eggs
½ cup molasses

½ cup sugar for coating

Sift together flour, salt, baking soda, ginger, cinnamon and cloves. Set aside.

In large bowl, beat together shortening, sugar and eggs until light and fluffy (about 2 to 3 minutes). Add molasses; blend. Add dry ingredients in small batches and mix using a spatula or heavy spoon until well blended. Refrigerate overnight.

Form into 1-inch balls and roll the balls of dough into ½ cup sugar. Place, spaced apart, on greased cookie sheet (or cookie sheet lined with parchment paper). Flatten and bake at 350°F for 10 to 15 minutes or until browned. Remove immediately and place on rack to cool.

> ✎ NOTE: *I tasted Carolyn Inouye's Gingersnap Cookies and they were so tasty and crisp I asked for the recipe. Carolyn is known for her delicious cookies. She uses 5 cookie sheets and fits 30 small cookies on each sheet. Instead of using butter as the original recipe called for, I used shortening for easier handling.*

Aggie's Oatmeal Cookies

Yield: 5 dozen

1 cup butter (2 blocks), softened
1 cup white sugar
1 cup brown sugar
2 eggs
1 teaspoon vanilla
1½ cups flour
1 teaspoon salt
1 teaspoon baking soda
3 cups oatmeal
1 cup nuts, chopped
1 cup raisins

Beat together butter and sugars until smooth and creamy. Add eggs one at a time; beating together. Add vanilla; beat together. In another bowl, sift together flour, salt and baking soda; add to butter mixture and mix together with large spoon or spatula. Add oatmeal, nuts and raisins; mix together. Drop about 1 heaping teaspoonful batter on ungreased cookie sheet and lightly press. Bake at 350°F for about 10 to 15 minutes. Check for doneness.

✍ SUGGESTION: *Bake 15 minutes for crispier cookies.*

✍ NOTE: *Aggie often shared her delicious home-baked cookies with others at St. Ann's Church. This was my favorite cookie. Aggie recommends that all ingredients be at room temperature before beginning and she also recommends beating butter and sugars together really well.*

Cookies & Bars

Apple Bars

Yield: 24 servings

CRUST:

4 cups flour
²/₃ cup sugar
1¼ cups butter (2½ blocks), cold

FILLING:

4 to 5 cups apples, diced (about 4 Granny Smith apples)
½ cup sugar
1½ teaspoons cinnamon
¼ cup flour

Mix together flour and sugar. Cut in cold butter until crumbly. Reserve 2 cups for topping, Press remaining dough into greased 9 x 13-inch pan. Set aside.

In large bowl, mix together apples, sugar and cinnamon. Add flour and mix thoroughly. Spread filling over crust. Sprinkle remaining crust mixture on top of filling. Bake at 375°F for 45 minutes or until golden brown.

> 🍰 HINT: *Cut butter into small cubes before adding to flour and cutting in until crumbly.*
>
> 🍰 NOTE: *Love this apple bar dessert! It's similar to apple crisp but it's easier to take to a potluck. The apples are fresh and not from a can.*

Apricot Bars

Yield: 30 to 36 bars

1⅓ cups dried apricots

Rinse apricots, cover with water and bring to boil; lower heat and simmer 10 minutes. Drain and set aside to cool.

CRUST:

2 cups flour
½ cup sugar
1 cup butter (2 blocks), chilled

Combine flour and sugar; cut butter into flour mixture until crumbly. Press mixture evenly into greased 9 x 13-inch pan. Bake at 350°F for 20 to 25 minutes. Set aside to cool.

While crust is cooling, chop apricots; set aside.

TOPPING:

4 eggs
2 cups brown sugar
1 teaspoon vanilla
⅔ cup flour
1 teaspoon baking powder
½ teaspoon salt
¾ cup walnuts or pecans, chopped (optional)
Powdered sugar, for sprinkling

In large bowl, beat eggs. Mix in brown sugar and vanilla. Add flour, baking powder and salt. Mix well. Stir in nuts and apricots. Spread mixture over cooled crust and bake at 350°F about 30 minutes, or until done. Cool in pan. Cut into bars and sprinkle with powdered sugar.

Jeri's Easy Trifle *(pg. 27)*

Mochi Muffins *(pg. 35)*

Hawaiian Sun® Chi Chi Dango *(pg. 136)*

Jell-O® Cream Cheese Pie *(pg. 68)*

Chocolate Crinkle Cookies *(pg. 94)*

Crispy Apricot Turnovers *(pg. 63)*

Tapioca (*pg. 145*)

Fruit Tart (*pg. 66*)

**Lemon Pie in
Meringue Shell**
(pg. 71)

Apple Bars *(pg. 83)*

Gingerbread Cookies
(pg. 104)

Cereal Almond Brittle *(pg. 129)*

Angel Tunnel Cake *(pg. 4)*

Christmas Confetti Cookies *(pg. 96)*

Brownies

Yield: 24 pieces

2 cups flour
2 cups sugar
1½ cups unsweetened cocoa
1 cup butter (2 blocks), melted
4 eggs, beaten
½ teaspoon vanilla
1 cup macadamia nuts, chopped

In large bowl, sift together flour, sugar and cocoa; mix. Add butter, eggs and vanilla; mix well. Pour into greased 9 x 13-inch pan. Top with nuts. Bake at 350°F for 35 to 40 minutes. Check for doneness. Do not over bake.

✎ **VARIATION:** *Top brownies with chocolate chips, if desired. Mix in chopped walnuts.*

✎ **NOTE:** *I met Ellen Fujihara at a pot luck party and she just happened to have this recipe from a friend in her purse. She had requested the brownie recipe after tasting it because it was so good. And knowing that I was working on a new dessert cookbook, she highly recommended this brownie recipe. A note on the recipe said, "North Kohala Favorites" 1991.*

Brownie Mochi

Yield: 24 to 30 servings

BROWNIE:

4 squares unsweetened chocolate (1 oz. each)
½ cup butter (1 block)
5 eggs, divided
1½ cups sugar
1½ teaspoons vanilla
¾ cup flour
½ teaspoon salt
1¼ cups pecans or walnuts, chopped and toasted (optional)

Melt butter and chocolate in saucepan over low heat; set aside. Beat eggs and divide in half (reserve the other half for mochi.) Beat eggs, sugar and vanilla for 5 to 10 minutes. Blend in chocolate mixture, flour and salt until just mixed. Stir in nuts. Pour into greased 9 x 13-inch pan. Set aside.

MOCHI:

½ pound mochiko (approximately 1½ cups and 1½ teaspoons)
1¼ cups sugar
1 teaspoon baking powder
¾ cup milk
Reserved half of eggs
¾ cup coconut milk
½ teaspoon vanilla
¼ cup butter (½ block), melted

Mix together mochiko, sugar and baking powder. Add rest of ingredients and blend well. Pour over brownie layer. Bake, uncovered, at 350°F for 35 to 40 minutes.

> 🥢 NOTE: *Sylvia Mitsui first tasted this concoction at a local bakery. It was originally in cupcake form and she liked it so she decided to create a similar treat. She made hers in a 9 x 13-inch pan which worked out quite well. To make it easier she says you can use any brownie recipe. Follow the box directions and just use 2 eggs for the mochi part.*

Cookies & Bars

Spice Shortbread Cookies

Yield: 8½ dozen

1 pound butter (4 blocks), softened
1¼ cup sugar
2 teaspoons vanilla

5 cups flour
2 to 3 teaspoons cinnamon
½ to ¾ teaspoon nutmeg
¼ teaspoon allspice (optional)

Beat butter and sugar until creamy; mix in vanilla. In another bowl, sift together flour, cinnamon, nutmeg and allspice, if desired. Add to butter mixture in small batches; using a spatula or heavy spoon, mix well.

Form into ¾- to 1-inch round balls. Place on ungreased cookie sheets and flatten to about ¼-inch thick or less. Prick several times with a fork and bake at 350°F for 14 to 18 minutes or until golden tan or brown. (The longer you bake, the crispier the cookies will be.)

✎ NOTE: *This is Jean Machida Bart's creation based on a recipe from Elaine Inouye. She was so generous to share it with us.*

✎ TIP: *Jean uses 3 trays at once in her convection oven which automatically reduces the temperature about 25°F. It takes from 22 to 28 minutes. I used a regular oven with a single tray and baked it for 17 minutes.*

Brownie-Raspberry Thumbprints

Yield: 4½ dozen

2 cups flour
1 teaspoon baking soda
¼ teaspoon salt
4 squares Baker's® Unsweetened Chocolate (1 oz. each)
½ cup butter (1 block)
1 box cream cheese (8 oz.)
1¼ cups sugar, divided
1 egg, beaten
1 teaspoon vanilla
⅓ cup raspberry jam

Mix flour, baking soda and salt; set aside.

Microwave chocolate and butter in large microwaveable bowl on high 2 minutes; stir until chocolate is completely melted. Whisk in cream cheese. Add 1 cup of the sugar, egg and vanilla; mix well. Stir in flour mixture. Refrigerate 15 minutes.

Roll dough into 1-inch balls; coat with remaining sugar. Place 2 inches apart on baking sheets. Press thumb into center of each ball; fill indentation with about ¼ teaspoon jam. Bake at 375°F for 10 to 12 minutes. Cool 1 minute on baking sheet; transfer to wire racks. Cool completely.

> ✎ **NOTE:** *Cookies are soft and cake-like. The flavor is great and not too sweet.*

Cookies & Bars

Butter Cookies

Yield: 5 dozen

1 cup butter (2 blocks), softened
1 cup sugar
2 eggs
1 teaspoon vanilla
2 cups flour
½ teaspoon cornstarch

Beat butter and sugar until fluffy. Add eggs, one at a time; beat to blend. Add vanilla. Sift flour and cornstarch together and add into wet ingredients; blend. Scoop teaspoonful of dough, form into balls and place on cookie sheet. Press fork tines into flour before lightly pressing down to flatten. Bake at 300°F for 18 to 20 minutes or until lightly browned. Remove immediately from cookie sheet and place on rack to cool. Store in airtight container.

> NOTE: *Agnes Leong shared this light and buttery cookie recipe and highly recommended it. The cookies were delicious! They were a perfect gift for an elderly friend who now lives in a care home.*

Chewy Cranberry Oatmeal Cookies

Yield: 4 dozen

1½ cups flour
1 teaspoon baking soda
½ teaspoon salt
½ teaspoon cinnamon
2½ cups rolled oats

1 cup unsalted butter (2 blocks), softened
1 cup light brown sugar, packed
½ cup white sugar
2 eggs
1 Tablespoon honey
2 teaspoons vanilla
1 package dried cranberries (6 oz., about 1⅓ cups cranberries)
1 cup macadamia nuts or walnuts, chopped

Lightly oil 2 to 3 cookie sheets or line them with parchment paper. In medium bowl, mix together flour, baking soda, cinnamon and oats; set aside.

In large bowl, beat butter and sugars with electric mixer until light and fluffy. Beat in eggs, one at a time. Add honey and vanilla; beat until blended. Add flour mixture in two batches, mixing with a wooden spoon until well blended. Stir in cranberries and nuts.

Drop the dough, one heaping teaspoon per cookie, about 2 inches apart on prepared baking sheet. Bake at 350°F about 10 to 12 minutes. (Bake until centers of cookies are soft, but no longer look wet.) Cool 5 minutes on baking sheet. Then transfer to rack to cool completely.

> 🖎 **NOTE:** *For a larger cookie use a heaping tablespoon. Bake longer if you prefer a crispier cookie.*

Chocolate Chip Oatmeal Cookies

Yield: 20 large cookies

1 cup butter (2 blocks), softened
1 cup light brown sugar
1 cup sugar
2 eggs

1½ cups flour
½ teaspoon salt
½ teaspoon baking powder
¼ teaspoon nutmeg
3 cups Quick-1 minute oats
1½ cups semisweet chocolate chips

In large bowl, beat butter and sugar until light and fluffy, about 3 minutes. Beat in eggs, one at a time. Set aside.

Adjust oven racks to low and middle positions; preheat oven to 350°F.

In another bowl, sift together flour, salt, baking powder and nutmeg and mix together. Add to butter mixture and stir with wooden spoon. Mix in oats and chocolate chips. Scoop out heaping tablespoonfuls of dough and form into balls. Place on parchment-lined cookie sheet and press lightly to flatten. Bake at 350°F for 22 to 25 minutes or until edges turn golden brown. (Halfway during baking, turn cookie sheet from front to back and switch from top to bottom rack.) Place cookies onto cooling racks.

Chocolate Biscotti Rounds

Yield: 3 dozen

½ cup butter (1 block), softened
1 cup sugar
1 egg
1½ teaspoons vanilla

1½ cups flour
½ cup unsweetened cocoa
½ teaspoon salt
½ teaspoon baking soda
½ teaspoon baking powder

½ cup sugar for coating

In large bowl, beat together butter, sugar, egg and vanilla until light and fluffy. Sift dry ingredients and add to butter mixture. Form into 1-inch balls and coat lightly with sugar. Place on lightly greased cookie sheet. Flatten dough slightly. Bake at 350°F for 12 to 14 minutes.

🍪 **VARIATION:** *Add ½ cup chopped walnuts if desired.*

🍪 **NOTE:** *Very tasty. Cookies are hard, biscotti-like.*

Chocolate Cranberry Cookies

Yield: 3½ dozen cookies

1 cup flour
½ cup unsweetened cocoa powder
1 teaspoon baking powder
¼ teaspoon salt

½ cup butter (1 block), softened to room temperature
1 cup sugar
1 egg
1 teaspoon instant coffee
1 teaspoon vanilla
½ cup semisweet miniature chocolate morsels
1 cup dried cranberries

In small bowl, sift together flour, cocoa, baking powder and salt; set aside.

In large bowl, beat butter and sugar on medium-high until light and fluffy. Beat in egg, coffee and vanilla; mix until smooth. Lower speed and beat in flour mixture just until combined. Stir in chocolate morsels and cranberries.

Drop dough by heaping teaspoons 2 inches apart on cookie sheets lined with parchment paper. Bake at 350°F for 10 to 12 minutes until tops are just firm. Cool on cookie sheet 2 minutes before transferring to wire rack.

> ✎ NOTE: *Chewy, with a slight taste of coffee in the chocolate. I used dried cranberries "with cherry juice infused" and I liked that cherry flavor. The amount of miniature chocolate morsels may be increased to 1 cup, if desired.*

Chocolate Crinkle Cookies

Yield: 4½ dozen

2 cups flour
2 teaspoons baking powder
½ teaspoon salt
4 ounces unsweetened chocolate
2 cups sugar
½ cup oil
4 eggs
2 teaspoons vanilla
Powdered sugar for coating

Sift together flour, baking powder and salt; set aside.

Place chocolate in large microwaveable bowl and heat for about 3 minutes to melt. Add sugar and oil; mix together. Blend in one egg at a time until mixed well. Add vanilla and flour mixture; mix well. Chill in refrigerator for several hours or overnight.

When chilled, place powdered sugar in bowl. Drop small teaspoonful of dough into the sugar. Roll and shape into a ball. Place about 2 inches apart on greased cookie sheet or parchment lined cookie sheet. Bake at 350°F for 10 to 12 minutes. As they bake and expand, the cookies will take on a crackly beautiful "snowy" look.

> ✎ **HINT:** *Use 2 teaspoons, one to scoop dough and the other to scrape off dough into powdered sugar. Dough will be easier to handle once it is covered with powdered sugar.*
>
> ✎ **NOTE:** *Pauline Masuda shared this recipe which she got from Maureen Beng who has had this recipe for over 40 years.*

Chocolate Shortbread

Yield: 8 dozen

1 pound butter (4 blocks), softened
1½ cups sugar
1 Tablespoon vanilla
5 cups flour
¾ cup cocoa powder
¼ teaspoon salt

Beat butter and sugar until light and fluffy; add vanilla. Sift together flour, cocoa powder and salt. Add in small portions to butter mixture. Use spatula to blend together. Form into balls and place on ungreased cookie sheets. Flatten and prick with fork times in 3 places. Bake at 350°F for about 20 to 25 minutes. (Do not over bake or cookies will burn.)

> ✎ NOTE: *This recipe was adapted by Jean Machida Bart based on an old Scotch Shortbread recipe from Elaine Inouye. Jean uses Hershey's dark cocoa powder but says if you want a milder flavor, use the regular cocoa powder.*

Christmas Confetti Cookies

Yield: 6 dozen cookies

1 cup butter (2 blocks)
1 cup sugar (or a little less)
2 Tablespoons milk
1 teaspoon vanilla
2½ cups flour
¾ cup red and green candied cherries, minced
½ cup macadamia nuts, finely chopped
¾ cup flaked coconut

Beat together butter and sugar until fluffy. Add milk and vanilla; beat well. Mix in flour, then cherries and nuts. Form into 2 rolls, 1½ inches in diameter. Roll in coconut. Wrap with waxed paper and chill several hours or overnight.

When ready to bake, slice rolls ¼-inch thick and place on ungreased baking sheets. Bake at 375°F for 10 to 12 minutes or until edges are golden brown.

Double Chocolate Brownie Cookies

Yield: 3 dozen cookies

1 box Ghirardelli Double Chocolate Brownie Mix® (18 oz.)
3 Tablespoons flour
½ cup butter (1 block), melted
2 eggs, lightly beaten
1 cup chocolate chips
1 cup macadamia nuts or walnuts, chopped

Mix flour into brownie mix. Add butter and eggs; mix. Add rest of ingredients; mix until combined. Place one tablespoonful of cookie dough onto cookie sheet. Bake at 350°F for 10 to 11 minutes. Let cookie rest in pan for 2 minutes before transferring to cooling rack.

Cocoa Krispies™ Chocolate Chip Cookies

Yield: 3½ dozen

1 cup unsalted butter (2 blocks), softened at room temperature
¾ cup sugar
1 teaspoon vanilla
2 cups flour, sifted
1 teaspoon baking soda
¼ teaspoon salt
1 cup semisweet chocolate chips
3½ cups chocolate crispy cereal (e.g. Kellogg's® Cocoa Krispies)

In large bowl, beat butter, sugar and vanilla on medium low for 2 to 3 minutes. In smaller bowl, combine flour, baking soda and salt; slowly add to butter mixture, beating on medium until blended. With rubber spatula or heavy spoon, mix in chocolate chips. Refrigerate dough 10 to 15 minutes for easier handling.

Scoop dough with teaspoon or small ice cream scooper and roll into a ball about an inch in diameter. Roll in cereal until cookie is well-covered. Place on ungreased cookie sheet. Place a sheet of waxed paper over cookies and flatten balls slightly using the bottom of a cup or can. Bake at 350°F for 18 to 20 minutes or until golden brown.

Cream Cheese Brownies

Yield: 24 brownies

1 box brownie mix (e.g. Duncan Hines® dark chocolate premium brownie mix (19.8 oz.), which requires 2 eggs, ⅓ cup vegetable oil and ⅓ cup water

CREAM CHEESE MIXTURE:

1 box cream cheese (8 oz.), softened
⅓ cup sugar
1 egg
½ teaspoon vanilla

Preheat oven to 350°F. Grease 9 x 13-inch pan.

Prepare brownie mix as directed on package; set aside.

In small bowl, beat cream cheese with sugar until well blended. Stir in egg and vanilla. Spread half of brownie batter in prepared pan. Cover with cream cheese mixture. Spread remaining brownie batter on top. Cut through batter with butter knife several times for marble effect. Bake for 20 to 25 minutes.

> ✎ **NOTE:** *One of T.J. Goodin's favorite! T.J. was a junior at MidPac when he shared this recipe with me. He often makes this for himself and his family.*

Crispy Chocolate Chip Cookies

Yield: about 8 dozen

1 cup butter (2 blocks), softened
1 cup sugar
½ cup brown sugar
2 eggs

2 cups flour
1 teaspoon baking soda
½ teaspoon baking powder
2 cups quick oatmeal
2 cups Rice Krispies®
2 cups macadamia nuts or walnuts, chopped
1 package semi-sweet chocolate chips (12 oz. or 2 cups)

Beat together butter and sugars until creamy. Add eggs; beat together.

Sift together flour, baking soda and baking powder and add to mixture; beat to blend together. Stir in oats, Rice Krispies®, nuts and chocolate chips. Scoop a heaping teaspoonful and form into balls; press lightly onto ungreased cookie sheet. Bake at 350°F for 12 to 15 minutes, or until done.

Drop Sugar Cookies

Yield: 3½ dozen cookies

2½ cups flour
¾ teaspoon salt
½ teaspoon baking soda
½ cup butter (1 block), softened
½ cup Crisco® vegetable shortening, softened
1 cup sugar
1 teaspoon vanilla
1 egg
2 Tablespoons milk

Sift flour, salt and baking soda together; set aside.

In large bowl, beat butter, shortening and sugar until light and fluffy. Add egg and vanilla; beat together. Add dry ingredients and beat until smooth. Blend in milk. Drop by tablespoonful about 3 inches apart on greased or parchment-lined cookie sheet. Bake at 350°F for 12 to 15 minutes or until lightly browned.

> ✎ **NOTE:** *For crispier cookies, press down slightly and flatten dough before baking.*
>
> ✎ **SUGGESTION:** *Decorate with colored icing. (See page 118 for cookie icing recipe.)*

Cookies & Bars

Easy Chocolate Bars

Yield: 24 servings

1 box yellow cake mix (18.25 oz.)
4 eggs, divided
½ cup butter (1 block), melted
6 Tablespoons cocoa(natural and unsweetened)
1 box powdered sugar (1 pound), or less if desired
1 box cream cheese (8 oz.), softened

Mix together cake mix, 1 egg and butter with wooden spoon; press down in bottom of 9 x 13-inch pan. Set aside.

Combine cocoa with remaining 3 eggs; beat at low speed. Add powdered sugar and cream cheese; beat until mixed well. Pour over cake mixture in pan. Bake at 350°F for 10 minutes. Reduce heat to 325°F and bake 35 minutes longer. Cool before cutting.

> NOTE: *After removing from oven, let light film of crust cool and "settle" before cutting. Tastes better the next day. This is definitely for chocolate lovers with a sweet tooth.*

Furikake Arare Cookies

Yield: 3½ dozen

2 cups flour
1 teaspoon baking soda
1 cup butter (2 blocks), softened
1 cup sugar
1 teaspoon vanilla
¼ cup nori kome furikake
1½ cups mini yakko arare

Sift together flour and baking soda; set aside.

In large mixing bowl, beat together butter and sugar about 2 to 3 minutes until fluffy. Mix in vanilla. Add flour mixture in two batches; mix until dough starts to come together. Do not overmix. Stir in furikake and arare. Cover with plastic wrap and chill dough about 20 minutes in refrigerator.

Preheat oven to 325°F and grease cookie sheets with nonstick cooking spray.

Drop dough by rounded teaspoons or small scoop onto baking sheet. Flatten slightly. Bake 15 to 18 minutes or until golden brown. Remove from oven and cool on cookie sheet about 10 minutes. Transfer cookies to wire rack to cool completely.

> 🍰 **NOTE:** *You may use any type of arare but pieces larger than mini yakko should be crushed.*

Garbage Cookies

Yield: 8 dozen

1 cup butter (2 blocks), softened to room temperature
1 cup sugar
1 cup brown sugar
2 eggs, beaten
1 teaspoon vanilla

2 cups flour
½ teaspoon baking powder
1 teaspoon baking soda
½ teaspoon salt
2 cups quick oatmeal
2 cups Rice Krispies® cereal
1 cup shredded coconut
1 cup nuts, chopped
1 cup chocolate chips

In large bowl beat butter and sugars until creamy. Add eggs and vanilla; beat together.

In separate bowl, sift flour, baking powder, baking soda and salt. Add to butter mixture and mix together.

Mix together oatmeal, Rice Krispies®, coconut, nuts and chocolate chips together; add to batter. Form into balls; press lightly onto ungreased cookie sheet. Bake at 350°F for 12 to 15 minutes.

> **NOTE:** *I met Betty Ikei at Safeway one early morning and we started to discuss recipes. She is such a friendly and generous person. Before I left the store she promised to give me some of her and her family's favorite recipes. Here is one of them. "Garbage Cookies" is an old, old family favorite. Someone must have named it so because of all the different ingredients that go into it.*

Gingerbread Cookies

Yield: 14 to 15 gingerbread men

2¼ blocks margarine, softened*
1½ cups sugar
½ cup molasses
2 small eggs, or medium eggs

5¼ cups flour
3 teaspoons baking soda
1¼ teaspoon cloves
1¼ teaspoon ginger
2 teaspoons cinnamon
½ teaspoon salt
Raisins, M&M's®, chocolate chips, icing, etc. to decorate

In large bowl, beat margarine and sugar until creamy. Add molasses; beat well. Add eggs, one at a time; beat well.

In another bowl, sift dry ingredients together and add to margarine mixture in small batches. Beat with beater on low speed. Mix with spatula or heavy spoon as dough thickens. Refrigerate 2 hours or overnight.

After refrigeration, form into 14 to 15 balls, about the size of a small orange. (If dough still seems too soft to handle, try sprinkling and mixing in more flour.) Refrigerate balls of dough until ready to use.

* Do not use Imperial® margarine or butter. Dough becomes too soft.

MAKING GINGERBREAD MEN WITH CHILDREN:

Provide a foil about 9-inches wide for each child. Use a permanent marker to write each child's name at the top in the middle of the foil. Give each child a ball of dough and have him follow your directions to create his own gingerbread man.

Divide the ball of dough into 4 parts. Roll into smooth balls.

Select the smallest piece for the gingerbread man's head. Form into a ball and place it directly under child's name. Press very firmly to flatten. (Flatten as much as possible to get a firmer cookie.)

For the body, select the largest piece. Shape into an oval and place it overlapping where the chin should be. Press to flatten.

Select the third piece and roll into stick shape. Break in half and press flat on body where arms should be. Do the same with last piece for the legs. Be sure to overlap and press each piece firmly onto body.

Decorate with raisins to make a mouth, M&M's® for eyes, chocolate chips, icing, etc.

Place each gingerbread man on foil onto cookie sheet. Trim or fold corners of foil to fit better. Bake at 375°F for 10 to 12 minutes or until done. Cool and give each child the gingerbread man he created. Each gingerbread man will be approximately 5 inches tall equivalent to 4 cookies.

> *NOTE: I did this activity with my kindergarten classes involving parents. Great fun and a great learning experience! One batch was done the night before. The second recipe was done at school in the morning with the children, refrigerated, and ready for each child to make his own gingerbread man in the afternoon.. The cookies were baked with help from the cafeteria staff. The children were so proud of their creations!*

This is a great activity for children and even for teenagers and certainly not limited to gingerbread men. Teenagers can be very creative. Any left-over dough can be rolled out on parchment paper, cut out with a cookie cutter and baked on parchment-lined cookie pans.

Kailua High School Shortbread Cookies

Yield: 25 squares

1 cup butter (2 blocks), softened
½ cup sugar
2⅓ cups sifted flour
¼ teaspoon salt

Beat butter; gradually add sugar and beat until light and fluffy. Combine flour and salt; mix into butter mixture until well combined and crumbly. Press evenly into greased 9-inch baking pan. Prick all over with fork. Bake at 300°F for 50 to 60 minutes or until golden brown. Cool slightly, cut into bars.

Easy Date Nut Bars

Yield: 24 to 30 pieces

1 box yellow cake mix (18.5 oz.)
¾ cup brown sugar
¾ cup butter (1½ blocks), melted
2 eggs, beaten
2 cups dates, chopped
2 cups walnuts, chopped

Preheat oven 350°F. Grease 9 x 13-inch pan.

Combine cake mix and brown sugar; blend well. Mix in eggs and butter. Add nuts and dates. (Batter will be stiff.) Spread batter evenly into greased pan. Bake for 35 to 45 minutes. Cool for 10 minutes. Cut into bars.

> **VARIATION:** *Add Craisins® or dried chopped apricots, if desired.*

Kathy's Chocolate Chip Cookies

Yield: 6 dozen

1 cup butter (2 blocks), softened to room temperature
1½ cups sugar
1 egg
2 teaspoons vanilla
2 cups flour
1 teaspoon baking soda
1 teaspoon salt
1 cup macadamia nuts, chopped coarsely
1 bag semi-sweet chocolate chips (12 oz.)

Beat together butter and sugar until creamy. Add egg; beat together. Add vanilla; beat together. Add flour, baking soda and salt and mix together with wooden spoon. Add nuts and chips and mix together. Scoop about a heaping teaspoonful batter and place on ungreased cookie sheet. Press down using bottom of flat glass dipped in flour. Bake at 350°F about 10 to 15 minutes, or until edges brown.

> ✎ **NOTE:** *Recipe from Evelyn Shiraki who got it from a friend of her son, Kevin, many years ago. These cookies are crispy and so tasty!*

M&M® Cookies

Yield: 12 dozen

2 cups butter (4 blocks), softened
2 cups brown sugar
1 cup sugar
4 eggs
1 Tablespoon vanilla
4½ cups flour
2 teaspoons baking soda
1 teaspoon salt
2 cups milk chocolate M&M's® candies (one 12.60 oz.bag)

Beat butter and sugar until light and fluffy. Beat in eggs and vanilla until thoroughly blended. Sift dry ingredients together. Gradually add sifted dry ingredients to butter mixture; blend together. Stir in M&M's® into cookie dough. Drop by teaspoonful onto lightly greased baking sheets. Bake at 350°F for 13 to 15 minutes.

Lemon Cheese Bars

Yield: 24 pieces

1 box lemon cake mix with pudding (15.25 oz.) e.g. Betty Crocker®
   Super Moist Lemon Cake made with pudding
2 eggs, divided
⅓ cup oil
1 box cream cheese (8 oz.), softened
¼ cup sugar
1 teaspoon lemon juice

Mix cake mix, 1 egg and oil until crumbly. Reserve 1 cup and press remaining cake mixture in ungreased 9 x 13-inch pan. Bake at 350°F for 15 minutes.

Beat cream cheese, sugar, 1 egg and lemon juice until light and smooth. Spread over baked layer. Sprinkle with reserved crumb mixture. Return to oven and bake for 15 to 20 minutes more. Cool; cut into bars.

Cookies & Bars

Lemon Cookies

Yield: 6 dozen

1 cup butter (2 blocks), softened
1 cup sugar
1 cup powdered sugar
1 cup vegetable oil
2 eggs
1 to 2 teaspoons lemon extract

4¾ cups flour
1 teaspoon baking soda
1 teaspoon salt
1 teaspoon cream of tartar

In large bowl, beat together butter and sugars until creamy. Beat in oil, eggs and lemon extract.

In another bowl, sift together flour, baking soda, salt and cream of tartar. Add to butter mixture and mix together until blended. Refrigerate 1 hour for easier handling. Scoop out rounded teaspoonfuls and roll into balls: place on cookie sheets. Bake at 350°F for 10 to 15 minutes, or until lightly browned.

> 🍰 **NOTE:** *Ellen Chew's 94 year old sister-in-law makes these cookies and they are so light and airy. They practically melt in your mouth.*

Liliko'i Bars

Yield: 24 to 30 bars

CRUST:

2 cups flour
½ cup powdered sugar
⅛ teaspoon salt
1 cup butter (2 blocks)

Combine flour, powdered sugar and salt; cut in cold butter until crumbly. Press onto bottom of lightly greased 9 x 13-inch pan. Bake at 300°F for 25 to 30 minutes or until golden brown. Remove from oven and turn oven up to 350°F.

TOPPING:

4 eggs, beaten
1½ cups sugar
1 teaspoon baking powder
3 Tablespoons flour
½ cup fresh liliko'i juice (adjust according to tartness)
¼ teaspoon lemon juice

While crust is baking, combine topping ingredients and mix well. Pour over baked crust (no need to let crust cool) and return to 350°F oven. Bake 20 to 25 minutes, or until golden brown. Cool about 25 minutes on wire rack and while still warm, loosen sides from pan and cut into bars using a wet knife. Sprinkle top with powdered sugar. Store in refrigerator.

> 🍪 **NOTE:** *Dr. Clayton Chong got this recipe after tasting it at a restaurant in Kona on the Big Island. Thank you, Dr. Chong for sharing it. (I now grow my own liliko'i so I can have fresh liliko'i juice handy. It grows very well on a chain link fence.)*
>
> 🍪 **HINT:** *Prepare a day before and refrigerate for best results. It tastes best chilled.*

Cookies & Bars

Norma's Cookies

Yield: 6½ dozen

1 pound butter (4 blocks), softened
1½ cups sugar
1 Tablespoon vanilla
4 cups flour
2 teaspoons baking soda

Beat together butter and sugar until light and fluffy. Mix in vanilla. Sift flour and baking soda and add in batches to butter mixture; mix to blend.

Select two or three of the following options to add to the batter.

OPTIONAL:

1 cup nuts
1 cup oatmeal
1 cup raisins or Craisins®
1 cup chocolate chips
1 cup Rice Krispies®

Scoop out dough and place on cookie sheet. Bake at 325°F for 20 to 25 minutes.

> ✎ NOTE: *Shared by Ruby Saito who got this delicious crispy recipe from Norma, a 1960 Roosevelt High School classmate. I especially like this recipe because you can make this cookie with whatever you have on hand.*

Oatmeal Crisp Cookies

Yield: 6½ dozen

1 cup butter (2 blocks), softened
1¼ cups sugar
2 egg yolks
2 cups flour
2 teaspoons baking soda
1¼ cups quick oatmeal
1 bag semi-sweet chocolate chips (12 oz.) or use less (about 1½ cups)
¾ cup macadamia nut bits

Beat butter and sugar until creamy; add egg yolks and beat together. Sift flour with baking soda and stir into batter. Add oatmeal and chocolate chips into batter. Add nuts; mix together. Roll into one inch balls (Do not flatten.) Place onto cookie sheets. Bake at 345°F for 10 to 15 minutes or until brown. Remove from oven and let cool on sheets slightly before removing.

> ✎ **NOTE:** *These cookies are really yummy and flaky! Be sure to use butter, not margarine.*
>
> ✎ **NOTE:** *Gwen Murai shared these delicious cookies at one of our Hilo High Class of '57 luncheons. She says you can leave the cookies in the oven longer if you want them browner and crispier. She begins with the 1st tray on the lower rack for 5 minutes or so until cookies expand. Then she moves it to the upper rack and puts the 2nd tray on the lower rack, etc.*

Cookies & Bars

Peanut Butter Cookies

Yield: 7 dozen

1 cup butter (2 blocks), softened
1 cup creamy peanut butter
1 cup sugar
1 cup packed brown sugar
2 eggs

2½ cups flour
1 teaspoon baking powder
1½ teaspoons baking soda
½ teaspoon salt (or use less)

In large bowl beat together butter, peanut butter, sugars. Add eggs and beat together thoroughly; set aside.

In another bowl, sift together flour, baking powder, baking soda and salt (dry ingredients). Add dry ingredients into butter mixture and mix thoroughly with wooden spoon. Chill dough for about one hour in refrigerator. Take out a small amount of chilled dough and roll dough into balls the size of large walnuts. Place onto ungreased baking sheets. Leave room for cookies to expand. Flatten crisscross fashion with fork dipped in flour. Bake at 325°F for 10 to 12 minutes or until brown.

> *NOTE: Measure flour by dip-level-pour method. Scoop up flour in measuring cup, level with butter knife sliding across rim and pour into sifter.*
>
> *NOTE: Gwen Murai contributed this crispy and tasty peanut butter cookie recipe. This is my favorite peanut butter cookie now!*

Peanut Butter Blossoms

Yield: 3½ dozen

½ cup sugar
½ cup brown sugar
½ cup butter (1 block), softened
½ cup peanut butter
1 egg
1 teaspoon vanilla
¼ teaspoon salt
1¾ cups flour
1 teaspoon baking soda
¼ cup sugar for coating
42 to 48 milk chocolate candy kisses, unwrapped

In large bowl, beat together ½ cup sugar, brown sugar, butter and peanut butter at medium speed until light and fluffy. Add egg, vanilla and salt; continue beating until well mixed. Add flour and baking soda. Beat, scraping bowl often, until well mixed.

Shape dough into 1-inch balls; roll in sugar to coat each cookie. Place onto ungreased cookie sheets about 2 inches apart. Press down slightly with flat surface. Bake at 375°F for 8 to 10 minutes or until golden brown. Remove from oven and immediately press 1 chocolate kiss in center of each cookie. Place on wire racks and cool completely.

> ☙ **TIP:** *If dough is too soft to shape into balls, refrigerate 30 to 60 minutes.*
>
> ☙ **NOTE:** *These cookies are pretty to look at and delicious. A Goodin family favorite. Kids will love them. Storage is a problem as they can't be stacked but they'll disappear quickly.*

Cookies & Bars

Janine's Favorite

Yield: 11 dozen

2 cups butter (4 blocks), softened to room temperature
2 cups white sugar
2 cups brown sugar
4 eggs
1 teaspoon vanilla

5 cups Old Fashioned Oatmeal
4 cups flour
1 teaspoon salt
2 teaspoons baking powder
2 teaspoons baking soda
3 cups Craisins® (or 1½ cup Craisins® and 1½ cup chocolate chips)
3 cups nuts, chopped

In large bowl, beat together butter and sugars until light and fluffy. Beat in eggs and vanilla; set aside.

Put small amounts of the oatmeal into a blender at a time, and blend until it turns to powder. In very large bowl, combine ground oats, flour, salt, baking powder and baking soda. Add butter mixture and mix together with a heavy spoon or strong spatula. Stir in Craisins® (or Craisins® and chocolate chips).

Scoop out tablespoonfuls and place on ungreased cookie sheet. Bake at 350°F for 12 minutes.

> 🥄 **VARIATION:** *For a softer cookie, bake at 375°F for 6 minutes. For those who prefer chocolate, substitute the Craisins® with 1 bag chocolate chips (24 oz.).*
>
> 🥄 **NOTE:** *Janine Baba shared this delicious cookie recipe. It makes a lot! I used my very large green Tupperware® container which was perfect for mixing everything.*

Potato Chip Cookies

Yield: 3½ dozen

1 cup unsalted butter (2 blocks)
½ cup sugar
Dash vanilla
1¾ cups flour
1¼ cups crushed potato chips
Powdered sugar for sprinkling (optional)

In large bowl, beat together butter and sugar until light and fluffy. Beat in vanilla. Add flour; blend. Mix in crushed potato chips. Chill for 30 minutes to firm dough for handling. Roll into 1-inch balls; place on cookie sheets and press down with a fork dipped in flour. Bake at 350°F for 15 minutes or until edges are brown. Sprinkle with powdered sugar.

> NOTE: *Very light and tasty with a slight crunch. (I placed 3 cookies in a cupcake baking cup wrapped them prettily and they were perfect for a little luncheon favor for a group of friends,) I also liked the cookies baked without pressing down, something like Russian Tea Cookies.*

Russian Tea Balls

Yield: 4 dozen

1 cup butter (2 blocks), softened
4 Tablespoons sifted powdered sugar
1 teaspoon vanilla
2 cups sifted flour
1 cup nuts, finely chopped
Sifted powder sugar for coating

In large bowl, beat butter and sugar until light and fluffy. Add vanilla; beat well. Add sifted flour in portions and beat well each time. Mix in nuts. Chill for 30 minutes or longer for easier handling.

Form into 1-inch balls and place onto ungreased cookie sheets. Bake at 350°F for 20 minutes or until edges are golden brown. Cool on brown paper bags. Roll and dust each cookie with sifted powdered sugar.

> 🍰 **NOTE:** *Flour should be sifted before measuring.*

Soft and Chewy Chocolate-Peanut Butter Cookies

Yield: 3½ dozen

1 box devil's food cake mix (18.25 oz.)
4 ounces Philadelphia cream cheese (half of 8 oz. package), softened
½ cup peanut butter
1 egg, slightly beaten

Place all ingredients in large bowl. Beat on low speed 2 minutes. Then beat on medium speed 2 minutes longer. Shape into 1-inch balls and place on baking sheets 2 inches apart. Flatten each ball with tines of fork dipped in sugar in criss-cross pattern. Bake at 375°F for 8 minutes or until edges of cookies are set. Cool 2 minutes on baking sheets. Remove to wire racks to cool completely.

> NOTE: *Very cake-like cookies. Expect cookies to be very soft.*

Cookie Icing

2 cups powdered sugar, sifted
4 teaspoons milk
4 teaspoons light corn syrup

Blend icing ingredients until smooth. Add more sugar or milk as needed for spreading consistency. Food color may be added, if desired.

Soft Molasses Cookies

Yield: 7 dozen

1¼ cups butter (2½ blocks), softened
1 cup brown sugar
½ cup honey
2 eggs
1 cup dark molasses
2 teaspoons baking soda
1 teaspoon cinnamon
½ teaspoon ground cloves
1 teaspoon salt
6 cups flour

Beat butter and sugar until creamy; add the rest of ingredients (except for flour) and mix together. Use heavy spoon to mix as you slowly add flour. Dough will be very thick. Chill overnight.

Spoon out large tablespoon of dough, roll into ball, place on ungreased cookie sheet and flatten with bottom of a glass, dipped in flour. Bake at 350°F about 10 to 15 minutes.

> ✎ **NOTE:** *Although cookies were meant to be soft, if you prefer crispier cookies, bake longer.*
>
> ✎ **SUGGESTION:** *Decorate with icing. Use store bought icing or use icing recipe on pg 118.*

Stone Cookies

Yield: 3½ dozen

4 cups flour
2 teaspoons baking soda
1 teaspoon baking powder
½ teaspoon salt

½ cup butter (1 block), softened
¼ cup oil
1½ cups sugar
3 eggs, beaten
¼ cup milk or water
2 teaspoons vanilla
Sugar for dusting

Sift flour, baking soda, baking powder and salt; set aside.

In large bowl, beat together butter, oil and sugar. Add eggs, milk and vanilla; beat together. Add dry ingredients and mix well. Chill for 1 hour for easier handling. Scoop out rounded tablespoonful of dough. Form into a ball and roll in sugar. Place onto parchment-lined or greased cookie sheet. Flatten with palm. Bake at 325°F for 25 minutes until golden brown and crisp.

> **NOTE:** *I also like it not so crispy and on the slightly chewy side. It reminds me of the Chinese soft cookies Goon Goon and Popo used to buy from Chinatown.*

Tsubushian Bars

Yield: 24 to 30 bars

CRUST:

1½ cups flour
¼ cup sugar
¾ cup butter (1½ blocks), chilled

In large bowl, combine flour and sugar; mix together. Cut in butter until mealy. Press mixture evenly into 9 x 13-inch pan. Bake at 350°F for 15 to 20 minutes or until slightly brown.

TOPPING:

½ cup flour
¾ cup sugar
1 teaspoon baking powder
¼ teaspoon salt
3 eggs, beaten
1 cup macadamia nuts (or walnuts), chopped
1 can tsubushian (red azuki bean paste) (18 oz.)

While crust is baking, combine flour, sugar, baking powder and salt in medium bowl. Mix in eggs until blended. Add nuts and tsubushian; mix together. Pour mixture over baked crust and bake additional 40 to 45 minutes. Cut into bars while warm; leave in pan to cool.

> ✎ **NOTE:** *At a church potluck several years ago, Henry Paolillo encouraged people to taste his wife's shortbread, saying that it's very good. I did, liked it very much and asked his wife, Vicky, for the recipe. The recipe above has a thinner crust than Vicky's original recipe since she mentioned that she prefers a thinner crust. I also reduced the amount of sugar from 1 cup to ¾ cup.*

Wholegrain Apricot-Pineapple Bars

Yield: 30 pieces

1 cup butter (2 blocks), softened
1 cup brown sugar
2 cups Quick-1 minute Quaker Oats®
1¾ cups flour
½ cup nuts, chopped
1 teaspoon cinnamon
¾ teaspoon salt
1 to 1½ cups apricot-pineapple preserves (or strawberry, raspberry, etc.)

In large bowl, beat butter and sugar. Add rest of ingredients (except preserves) and beat at low speed until mixture is crumbly. Reserve 2 cups mixture. Press remaining mixture onto bottom of greased 9 x 13-inch pan. Spread preserves evenly over. Sprinkle remaining reserved mixture. Bake at 350°F for 30 to 45 minutes or until golden brown. Cool before cutting bars.

> ✎ **SUGGESTION:** *Substitute with other preserves of your choice.*

Assorted
Treats

Almond Float

Yield: 12 servings

3 envelopes unflavored gelatin
3 cups water, divided
1 cup evaporated milk
1 cup sugar
4 teaspoons almond extract
1 to 2 cans mandarin oranges (15 oz. each), or other fruits of your
   choice

Dissolve gelatin in 1 cup of the water. Heat evaporated milk, 2 cups water and sugar; add gelatin and stir until sugar and gelatin are dissolved. Cool and add almond extract. Pour into 9 x 13-inch pan and refrigerate to set. Cut into cubes and place in serving bowl. Pour mandarin oranges over, including syrup. (If using 2 cans of mandarin oranges, drain second can.)

> ✎ **NOTE:** *A very refreshing dessert! Everyone's favorite and it is one of the easiest desserts to make. For softer texture, add 3 Tablespoons more water when dissolving gelatin.*

Almond Roca Bars

Yield: 72 pieces

1 box Original Hawaiian Graham Crackers® from Diamond Bakery
1 cup butter (2 blocks)
½ cup sugar
¾ cup slivered almonds, chopped

Line 2 cookie sheets with non-stick aluminum foil. Lay crackers in rows. Melt butter and sugar together until bubbly. (Remove from heat at the slightest bubble.) Spoon or use pastry brush to coat hot mixture evenly over crackers. Be sure to saturate crackers. Sprinkle nuts over crackers. Bake at 325°F for 7½ minutes then turn cookie sheet and continue baking for additional 7½ minutes until slightly brown.

> ✎ NOTE: *Do not use margarine. Baking time may vary depending on oven. Watch carefully. Do not burn bottom. You may need to adjust baking time or temperature. Jan Uesato, who emailed the recipe to me, usually buys slivered almonds from Trader Joe's and uses a food processor to chop them. She freezes the almonds and uses them as needed.*
>
> ✎ HINT: *Almond Roca Bars may be frozen to be consumed later.*

Apple Crisp

Yield: 20 servings

4 cups flour
1 cup sugar
1½ cups butter (3 blocks), chilled
2 cans Comstock® More Fruit Apple Pie Filling (21 oz. each)
2 teaspoons cinnamon

Mix flour and sugar together in large bowl. Cut cold butter into flour until the consistency is crumbly.

Sprinkle ¾ of the flour mixture evenly in 9 x 13-inch greased pan. (Do not press down.) Spoon apple pie filling evenly over flour mixture. Mix cinnamon into the remaining flour mixture. Sprinkle on top of apple layer. Bake at 350°F for 1 hour. Let stand for 10 minutes before serving.

> 🍰 **NOTE:** *After baking, if desired, turn on broiler and broil for 1 to 2 minutes until golden brown. Watch to see that it doesn't burn. Jennifer Nakamura served this at a get-together with her friends. My daughter really enjoyed it and recommended it for this cookbook. Very easy to make.*
>
> 🍰 **SUGGESTION:** *Serve with vanilla ice cream or whipped cream. Yummy!*

Avocado-Lime Jell-O®

Yield: 20 servings

1 large box lime or lemon Jell-O® (6 oz.)
½ cup sugar
2 cups boiling water

In medium bowl, mix together lime Jell-O®, sugar and boiling water. Set aside to cool.

2 envelopes Knox® gelatin
½ cup water
½ cup mayonnaise
½ cup milk
¾ to 1 cup avocado, mashed

Mix together gelatin and water; set aside.

In small bowl, blend together mayonnaise, milk and avocado. Add gelatin mixture; blend. Add to Jell-O®; mix together. Pour into 9 x 9-inch pan well-rubbed with mayonnaise. Chill well.

> ✎ **NOTE:** *I had given Kathryn Kato some avocados from my tree and she later emailed this avocado recipe to me. Her sister had made this avocado dessert and she said it's quite good.*
>
> ✎ **TIP:** *Avocado pulp can be frozen and it works well for this recipe. Scoop out enough avocado for 1 cup and seal in baggies for future use.*

Banana Mochi

Yield: 24 to 30 servings

1 box mochiko (16 oz.)
3 teaspoons baking soda
1 cup unsalted butter (2 blocks), softened
1½ cups sugar
4 eggs
1 can coconut milk (12 oz.)
1 can evaporated milk (12 oz.)
2 teaspoons vanilla
3 large ripe bananas, mashed (Do not use apple bananas)

In large bowl, combine mochiko and baking soda; set aside.

In another bowl, beat butter and sugar. Beat in eggs, one at a time. Mix in coconut milk, evaporated milk and vanilla; blend well. Gradually add liquid mixture into dry ingredients using a whisk or heavy spoon to blend well. Fold in bananas. Pour into ungreased 9 x 13-inch pan.

Bake at 350°F for 1 hour or until center is baked. Let set 8 to 12 hours or overnight, covered with dishtowel.

Jell-O ® Kanten

Yield: 20 pieces

1 large box strawberry Jell-O® (6 oz.), or use lime or orange flavor
4 envelopes Knox® gelatin
½ cup sugar (or a little less)
5 cups water (½ cup tap water and 4½ cups hot water)

Pour ½ cup tap water into large bowl. Add Jell-O®, gelatin and sugar; mix to make a paste. Pour hot water into mixture, stir to blend. Cool.

Pour into 9 x 9-inch pan slightly greased with mayonnaise. Refrigerate to set.

> ✎ **VARIATION:** *Add drained diced peaches and/or lychee. Refrigerate Jell-O® for ½ hour first before adding in fruits.*

Cereal-Almond Brittle

Yield: 14 servings

2 cups Cheerios® cereal
2 cups Cinnamon Toast Crunch® cereal
2 cups quick oats
1 cup almonds, sliced
½ cup butter
¼ cup brown sugar, packed
⅓ cup maple syrup, real or maple-flavored

Line large 17 x 14-inch cookie sheet (or two 10 x 15-inch pans) with "no stick" foil. Spray foil with cooking spray. In large bowl, mix both cereals, oats and almonds; set aside.

In saucepan, heat butter, brown sugar and syrup over medium heat, stirring frequently, until mixture boils. Pour over cereal mixture and stir until well coated. Spread mixture evenly on cookie sheet with rubber spatula until about ½-inch thick.

Bake at 300°F for 35 to 40 minutes or until almonds are golden brown. Cool completely, about 15 minutes. Break into pieces with fingers. Store in tightly covered container.

> ✎ NOTE: *Kathryn Kato raved about this snack and wanted to share it with me. It was quite easy to make. I loved it and I couldn't stop eating it. It is so good!*

Cocoa Mochi

Yield: 30 pieces

2 cups mochiko
1¾ cups sugar
1 Tablespoon baking soda
3 Tablespoons Hershey's® cocoa
2 eggs
1 can evaporated milk (12 oz.)
1 can coconut milk (13.5 oz.)
1 teaspoon vanilla

In large bowl, sift together dry ingredients. In another bowl, beat eggs and add rest of wet ingredients; mix together.

Make a "well" in center of the dry ingredients. Pour milk mixture into dry ingredients and stir, beginning from center. Mix until batter is smooth. Pour into well-greased 9 x 13-inch pan and bake at 350°F for 1 hour or until done. Completely cool before cutting with plastic knife.

> ✎ NOTE: *Nancy Len shared this recipe which is a variation of the original cocoa mochi recipe. She eliminates butter in her recipe and the mochi becomes less cake-like and has a smoother texture. Very delicious! She said she also substitutes skim evaporated milk and egg substitute with good results.*

Cocoa Mochiko Cake

Yield: 28 servings

1¾ cups sugar
2 Tablespoons dark ground cocoa
   (e.g. Hershey's® Special Dark Cocoa)
2 Tablespoons natural unsweetened cocoa
1 Tablespoon baking soda
1 box mochiko (1 pound)

½ cup butter (1 block), melted
1⅔ cups milk
1 can coconut milk (12 oz.)
3 eggs, beaten

In large bowl, sift sugar, cocoa powders and baking soda. Add mochiko and mix together; set aside.

In smaller bowl, mix butter, milk, coconut milk and eggs. Make a "well" in the large bowl of dry ingredients and gradually stir wet mixture into dry ingredients. Mix thoroughly to remove any lumps. Pour into greased 9 x 13-inch pan and bake at 350°F for 1 hour. Turn off heat and leave in oven for 15 minutes. Remove and cool on rack. Use plastic knife to cut into pieces.

> ✎ **NOTE:** *This version is darker, richer and smoother. I am amazed at how many variations there are. But here in Hawai'i we seem to like anything with mochi. It tastes great and is so easy to prepare.*

Coconut Red Bean Mochi

Yield: 30 servings

2½ cups mochiko
1 can coconut milk (13.5 oz.)
½ cup whole milk
½ cup water
½ teaspoon salt
3 Tablespoons light corn syrup
1 teaspoon sugar
2 eggs, beaten
1 can Koshian (13.5 oz.)

EGG WASH:

1 egg yolk and 2 tablespoons milk beaten together

Preheat oven 350°F.

In large mixing bowl, whisk together mochiko, coconut milk, milk, water and salt until well-blended. Stir in light corn syrup, sugar and eggs.

Pour about two thirds of mochiko batter into 9 x 13-inch pan. Place small dollops of koshian in an even layer over the batter. Cover with remaining batter. Lightly brush on egg wash. Bake for 60 to 65 minutes, or until golden brown in color. Cool thoroughly before cutting with plastic knife.

> 🍃 NOTE: *Very soft and tasty. Recipe was shared by my good friend, Miriam Tango Cooney, who got it from Betty Sasaki. Although living on the mainland now, both grew up in Hilo and they still enjoy the taste of mochi. Please note that the koshian can called for is 13.5 oz. which is difficult to find in stores today. Please adjust accordingly to the amount used.*

Assorted Treats

Coffee Azuki Gelatin

Yield: 20 servings

2½ cups hot coffee
1 can sweetened condensed milk (14 oz.)
4 envelopes unflavored gelatin
½ cup strong cold coffee
1 can tsubushian (18 oz.)
¼ teaspoon salt

Combine hot coffee and condensed milk; mix.

Soften gelatin in cold coffee. Add it to the milk mixture and stir until gelatin is dissolved. Add tsubushian and salt; mix thoroughly. Pour into 9 x 9-inch pan. Refrigerate until firm.

> ✎ NOTE: *If you like sweetened coffee you will enjoy this. Very cool and refreshing. Shared by Ruby Saito.*

Bread Pudding

Yield: 9 servings

6 slices day old bread, cut into 1 inch cubes
4 eggs, beaten
2 cups milk
¾ cup sugar (or less)
2 tablespoons butter, melted
1 teaspoon vanilla
⅓ cup raisins
1 teaspoon cinnamon

Place bread cubes in greased 8 x 8-inch pan.

Combine eggs, milk, sugar, butter and vanilla. Pour over bread cubes. Press bread cubes into milk mixture to soak all pieces. Place raisins over and sprinkle cinnamon over all. Bake at 350°F for 45 minutes.

Cream Cheese Kanten

Yield: 20 servings

1 box cream cheese (8 oz.), softened
1 cup sugar (or less)
4 envelopes Knox® gelatin
¼ cup water
1¼ cups hot water
3 cans mandarin oranges (11 oz. each), drained
1 can 7-Up® or Sprite®

Lightly grease 9 x 9-inch pan.

In small bowl, dissolve gelatin with ¼ cup water. Add 1¼ cups hot water to the dissolved gelatin and stir well to blend.

In large bowl, beat cream cheese and sugar. Stir gelatin mixture slowly into cream cheese mixture; blend thoroughly. Mix in fruit and 7-Up®. Ladle liquid and fruit evenly into pan. Refrigerate to set.

> 🥄 NOTE: *Shared by Betty Oishi, a retired grandmother. She often makes this for family and church gatherings. The kanten is refreshing and stays firm while being served at a potluck.*
>
> 🥄 VARIATION: *My granddaughters like mandarin oranges but their Tai Tai prefers peaches. Substitute mandarin oranges with 2 cans lite sliced peaches (15 oz. each), cut in large chunks.*

Assorted Treats

Fuji Apple Bread Pudding

Yield: 24 servings

9 eggs
1¾ cups sugar
1 teaspoon cinnamon
1 teaspoon vanilla
½ teaspoon salt

2 cans evaporated milk (12 oz. each)
3 cups water
½ cup butter (1 block)
1 King's Hawaiian® sweet bread, cubed
½ to 1 cup raisins
2 Fuji apples

In medium bowl, beat eggs with whisk. Add sugar, cinnamon, vanilla and salt; mix thoroughly. Set aside.

Heat evaporated milk, water and butter until butter melts. Remove from heat; cool slightly. Combine egg mixture into milk mixture.

Cut apples into fourths. Core, peel and slice thinly. In large bowl, combine bread, raisins and apples. Pour milk mixture over. Gently mix together and let soak in refrigerator at least 30 minutes. Pour into greased 9 x 13-inch pan and bake at 325°F for 1 hour and 5 minutes.

> ✎ NOTE: *Refrigerate any leftover bread pudding. It tastes even better the next day, especially with a hot cup of coffee.*

Hawaiian Sun®
Chi Chi Dango

Yield: 9 x 9-inch pan

- 3 cups mochiko
- 1 cup sugar
- 2 packages Hawaiian Sun® powdered juice mix (4.52 oz. each)
  e.g. pineapple-orange
- 2 cans evaporated milk (12 oz. each)
- ½ cup water
- 4 drops food color (mix of yellow and red)
- 1 package katakuriko (potato starch) (10 oz.), for dusting

Combine all ingredients (except katakuriko); mix with heavy spoon until smooth. Pour into greased 9 x 9-inch pan and bake, uncovered, at 350°F for 55 to 60 minutes or until center is set. Cool in pan overnight. Use plastic knife to slice into pieces. Coat with katakuriko to prevent sticking. Use pastry brush to brush off excess katakuriko.

> ✎ HINT: *To cut mochi, use a lot of potato starch. Divide pan into 4 long strips. Use a plastic knife and fingers to loosen and carefully lift one strip out. Place on cutting board dusted with potato starch.*
>
> ✎ NOTE: *My cousin's wife, Barbara Fuchigami, shared this with me after she had tasted the mochi at a party and requested the recipe. I made 3 different flavors for a luncheon and everyone liked the taste and chewy texture.*
>
> ✎ SUGGESTION: *Try these flavors.*
>
> - *2 packages Liliko'i Passion (4.16 oz. each) and 3 drops yellow food color*
>
> - *2 packages Guava Nectar (3.23 oz. each) and 6 drops red food color*

Lemon Mochi

Yield: 24 to 30 servings

1 box mochiko (16 oz.)
2¼ cups sugar
4 teaspoons baking powder
1 box instant lemon pudding (3 oz.)
3 cups milk
½ cup butter (1 block), melted
5 eggs, lightly beaten
2 teaspoons lemon extract
1 cup angel-flake sweetened shredded coconut

In large bowl, stir together mochiko, sugar, baking powder and instant pudding mix. Make a well in middle and gradually whisk in milk to smooth out lumps. One at a time, stir in melted butter, beaten eggs, lemon extract and coconut. Pour into greased 9 x 13-inch pan. Bake at 350°F for 1 hour or until inserted toothpick or skewer comes out clean.

> ✎ **VARIATION:** *Instead of 3 cups milk, use 1 can coconut milk (14.5 oz.) and add milk to make 3 cups.*

Liliko'i Pudding
with Tapioca Pearls

Yield: 8 servings

½ cup small tapioca pearls
1 cup warm water
2 cups water
Pinch salt
1 can coconut milk (13 oz.)
½ cup sugar
½ teaspoon vanilla
3 Tablespoons liliko'i juice
1 can fruit cocktail (8.5 oz.), drained (or 1 cup chopped fresh fruit)

Rinse and drain tapioca pearls once. Then soak tapioca in warm water 30 minutes.

In medium saucepan, bring 2 cups water and salt to boil. Add tapioca with soaking water. Reduce heat to medium-low and cook 5 to 8 minutes, stirring frequently, until most of the pearls turn from white to translucent. Add a little more water if too thick and sticky.

Add coconut milk and return to boil. Reduce heat, add sugar and stir to dissolve. Cook another 5 minutes to thicken slightly. Remove from heat; add vanilla. Cover and let sit 30 minutes.

Stir in liliko'i. Taste and add more sugar or liliko'i juice to your taste. Pour into bowl or divide into dessert cups. Chill until firm.

Pour a little juice over pudding and top with fruit.

Assorted Treats

Local Style Fruit Cocktail #1

Yield: 6 to 8 servings

3 cups jabon, peel and break flesh apart into bite-sized pieces
1 can whole lychees (20 oz.), drain but reserve liquid
1 can mandarin oranges (15 oz.), drain but reserve liquid

Combine fruits in large bowl and toss gently. Add desired amount of lychee and mandarin liquid to fruits. Serve chilled.

> ✎ NOTE: *My friend, Kathryn Kato gave me a beautiful jabon and suggested this refreshing fruit cocktail. Jabon (Japanese) is also known as bulok (Chinese) and in English as pomelo. She said that even people who don't care for jabon like this fruit cocktail.*

Local Style Fruit Cocktail #2

Yield: 6 to 8 servings

3 cups jabon, peel and break flesh apart into bite-sized pieces
1 can pineapple chunks in heavy syrup (20 oz.),
    drain but reserve juice
1 container sliced frozen strawberries with sugar (16 oz.),
    including juice

Combine fruits in large bowl and toss gently. Add desired amount of pineapple juice for desired consistency.

> ✎ NOTE: *Leilani Hoshide Matoba brought jabon to our '57 class luncheon to share with us and suggested this tasty and beautiful presentation.*

Peanut Butter Balls

Yield: 34 to 36 balls

½ cup sugar
1 cup Karo® light corn syrup
1 jar peanut butter (18 oz.) e.g. Reese's® creamy peanut butter
 (1 lb. 2 oz.)
4½ cups Rice Krispies®
1 cup raisins or Craisins® (or combination of both)
1 package Hershey's® Kisses candy (9 oz.)

BEFORE BEGINNING:

Scoop out peanut butter from jar into small bowl for easier handling.

Unwrap 36 candy Kisses and have ready to put into center of ball.

Spread a length of waxed paper in 9 x 13-inch pan for balls to cool on.

Heat sugar and Karo® syrup in large pot, first at medium low, then at medium heat, stirring constantly. Bring to boil and remove from heat. Immediately add peanut butter; stir until blended and smooth.

Add Rice Krispies® and raisins and mix thoroughly. Be sure all dry ingredients are coated with peanut butter mixture. (Add more Rice Krispies®, if necessary.) Work quickly as it gets harder as it cools. Use thin disposable gloves to keep mixture from sticking to your hands.*

Scoop a heaping tablespoonful of cereal mixture, make a hole in the center and insert a Kiss, pointed end down, and cover by bringing cereal mixture over. Add more cereal mixture as needed to cover. Place balls on waxed paper. Cool before wrapping. Wrap with 6 x 8-inch pieces of waxed paper. Roll each ball in waxed paper and twist ends.

*I found Playtex® Clean Cuisine disposable gloves for handling food at Long's® and they worked very well.

> ✎ NOTE: *This snack was shared by Japan tour leader, Lionel Tashiro. It was made by his wife, Janice. Everyone enjoyed it on the long bus ride. The balls last for days without refrigeration.*

Pineapple Cranberry Jell-O ®

Yield: 16 servings

2 boxes raspberry Jell-O® (3 oz. each)
1¼ cups hot water
1 can whole berry cranberry sauce (16 oz.)
1 can crushed pineapple (20 oz.), undrained
¾ cup apple juice

TOPPING:

1 box cream cheese (8 oz.), softened
1 cup sour cream
½ to 1 cup walnuts, chopped

In large bowl, dissolve Jell-O® in boiling water. Stir in undrained pine-apple, cranberry sauce and apple juice. Pour into 9 x 9-inch pan. Refrigerate to set, about 8 hours.

Beat cream cheese and sour cream until smooth. Spread over Jell-O® and sprinkle nuts over.

🥄 **VARIATION:** *Fold nuts into Jell-O®, if desired.*

🥄 **HINT:** *Refrigerate Jell-O® overnight and finish in the morning.*

Pistachio Fruit Dessert

Yield: 30 servings

STEP 1:

2 containers small curd cottage cheese (16 oz. each)
1 can crushed pineapple (20 oz.), drained really well until almost
   no juice left
2 containers Cool Whip® (8 oz. each)
1 box instant pistachio pudding (3.4 oz.)

In large container, begin with mixing cottage cheese and crushed pineapple. Mix in Cool Whip®, then the instant pistachio pudding powder. Mix together. Refrigerate 6 hours or overnight to firm.

STEP 2:

2 boxes lime Jell-O® (3 oz. each)
2 cups hot water

Combine lime Jell-O® with 2 cups hot water. Pour into 8 x 8-inch pan and refrigerate until firm.

STEP 3:

1 can pineapple chunks (20 oz.), drain well
2 cans mandarin orange (11 oz.), drain well
1 can sliced peaches (15 oz.), cut into cubes, drain well

Add fruits to chilled and firm cottage cheese mixture and mix together. Cut Jell-O® into cubes; add to cottage cheese mixture. Mix lightly so Jell-O® cubes do not break apart. Refrigerate until ready to serve.

🥄 **VARIATION:** *Add coconut flakes and mini marshmallows, if desired.*

🥄 **NOTE:** *This makes a lot! So plan to serve it at a large gathering. I have had so many requests for this recipe which I got from Gwen Murai who got it from Carolyn Kotomori when she served it at one of our reunion meetings.*

Assorted Treats

Rice Krispies®
with Furikake & Mochi Crunch

Yield: 30 pieces

½ cup butter (1 block)
5 cups Rice Krispies®
¼ cup Nori Komi Furikake
1 package mini yakko mochi crunch (8 oz.)
1 package large marshmallows (10 oz.)

Grease 9 x 13-inch pan; set aside.

In large pot, melt butter on low heat. While butter is melting, mix together Rice Krispies®, furikake and mochi crunch in large bowl; set aside.

Add marshmallow to melted butter, stirring constantly, until melted. Remove from heat and quickly add cereal mixture. Mix until all pieces are coated. Place mixture into pan and press evenly with back o f wooden spoon or press down using a good sized piece of foil.

When cool and set, cut into pieces and wrap individually in waxed paper for easier handling.

> ✒ **NOTE:** *It takes a little getting used to the taste but for those who like the sweet/salty combo taste it's quite good. I got to like it myself. Thanks to Gwen for sharing this very local-style treat.*

Prune Mui

Yield: 12 cups

6 packages pitted prunes (10 oz.)
2 packages dried apricots (6 oz.)

SAUCE:

1½ cups lemon juice
1 box brown sugar (1 pound)
3 Tablespoons Hawaiian salt
1 Tablespoon 5-spices
3 Tablespoons whiskey
2 Tablespoons honey, optional
1 teaspoon ground cloves (or 10 whole cloves)
1 package dried lemon peel (3 oz.), cut into strips and discard seeds
1 package seedless ling hing mui (4 oz.), shredded

Mix together sauce ingredients in large container; add dried fruits. Mix together thoroughly. Continue to mix in the morning and at night for 4 to 6 days to marinate fruits evenly.

> 🥄 NOTE: *Love this prune mui! The taste is super delicious. I combined almost identical recipes from Jane Danstuka and Joan Sato for this version. Jane uses one more ingredient which I could not find anywhere, She uses a sprinkle of see moi type red ginger. Jane makes this prune mui to give away for Christmas and I was so fortunate to be there having coffee at Ala Moana when she gave a container to me. Thank you, Jane.*

Tapioca Dessert

Yield: 15 servings

1 cup small tapioca pearls*
7 cups water
1¼ cups sugar
1 bag frozen Hawaiian Sun® Coconut Milk (12 oz.), thawed
2½ cups fresh or canned fruits (mango, lychee, honeydew melon, nectarine, etc.), cut in small pieces

Boil 7 cups water in non-stick pot. Add tapioca pearls; stir well. (Be sure pearls are all covered by water.) Boil gently, uncovered, for 15 to 20 minutes until pearls become translucent. Stir frequently to avoid pearls sticking to bottom of pot.

Turn heat off. Cover and let sit 30 minutes. Add sugar. Cool. When cool, add coconut milk and mix well. Add fruits; refrigerate.

*Small tapioca pearls may be found at Times Super Market (Reese® small pearl tapioca) or at Don Quijote (Cock® brand small tapioca pearls).

NOTE: *Super refreshing!*

WARNING: *Do not use Kraft® Minute Tapioca.*

Glossary

AN PASTE	made from beans, made to fill confections
ARARE	rice crackers
AZUKI	small red beans
CHI CHI DANGO	milk dumpling
FURIKAKE	rice condiment
HAUPIA	coconut cornstarch pudding
JABON	Japanese name for pomelo fruit or bulok (Chinese)
KANTEN	agar agar, made of seaweed that jells at room temperature*
KATAKURIKO	potato starch
KOSHIAN	smooth bean paste
LING HING MUI	preserved and seasoned Chinese plums (also spelled li hing mui)
LILIKO'I	passion fruit
MOCHI	glutinous rice or sweet rice floor
MOCHI CRUNCH	arare, rice crackers
MOCHIKO	glutinous rice flour
PRUNE MUI	prunes seasoned with Chinese spices
TSUBUSHIAN	coarsely ground red bean paste

*The use of the word "kanten" in this cookbook refers to the consistency of the Jell-O® desserts that can remain firm at room temperature by using Knox® gelatin.

Recipe Index